Teacher Reso

CW01597446

MATHS ACTIVITIES

Key Stage 2/P4-P7

Book 2

BRIGHTER VISION ®

Brighter Vision Education Ltd.,
Eton House, 18-24 Paradise Road, Richmond, Surrey TW9 1SR

Some material used in this edition is used under licence from
Frank Schaffer Publications Inc.

Consultant Editor: Pam Hutchinson

BV-05-310 Teacher Resource Maths Activities Key Stage 2/P4-P7 Book 2
ISBN 1 86172 160 9

Introduction

This set of 98 maths activities has been designed as further practice and consolidation materials for Key Stage 2 pupils and Scottish Curriculum Years P4 to P7. This is the second of two maths resource books for use at Key Stage 2 / P4-P7 and is particularly suitable for children in Years 5 and 6; the first book contains activities which will be of value to pupils in Years 3 and 4. Both books contain a balance of challenges and reinforcement material.

The contents list gives information about skills covered in each activity and this information is repeated on the separate photocopiable sheets. The skills covered are organised under the following headings:

★ Number
★ Addition
★ Subtraction
★ Addition and Subtraction
★ Multiplication
★ Division
★ Multiplication and Division
★ Fractions and Decimals
★ Measurement
★ Shape
★ Data Handling
★ Problem Solving

Each activity is free-standing and may be used alongside any course materials; the sheets provide enjoyable, motivating exercises which are ideal for taking home for extra practice and extension work.

Contents

Number

Place value - millions 1
Place value - millions 2
Comparing Numbers 3
Rounding Numbers 4
Highest common factor 5
Estimating sums and differences 6
Estimating sums and differences 7
Roman numerals .8

Addition

Two- and three-digit addends, regrouping 9
Two- and three-digit addends, regrouping 10
Two- and three-digit addends, regrouping 11
Three-digit addends, no regrouping . . .12
Three-digit addends, regrouping 13
Three-digit addends, regrouping 14
Four-digit addition 15
Four-digit addition 16

Subtraction

Subtracting multiples of 10 17
Two-digit subtraction, no regrouping . . .18
Two-digit subtraction, regrouping 19
Two-digit subtraction, regrouping 20
Two-digit subtraction, regrouping 21
Three-digit subtraction, regrouping 22
Three-digit subtraction, regrouping 23
Three-digit subtraction, regrouping 24
Three-digit subtraction, with/without regrouping 25
Two-to-five digit subtraction 26
Four-digit subtraction 27

Addition and Subtraction

Addition and subtraction, three-and four-digit numbers 28
Addition and subtraction, three-four and five-digit numbers 29

Multiplication

Multiplication facts, 0-9 as factors 30
Multiplication facts, 0-10 as factors 31
Multiplying 1-9 as factors 32
Multiplying by 5 and 6 33
Multiplying by 5, 6, 7, 8 and 9 34
Multiplying by 7 and 8 35
Multiplying by 9 and 10 36
Multiplying by multiples of 10 37
Multiplying by multiples of 100 38
Multiplying two-digit by one-digit numbers, regrouping 39
Multiplying by two-digit numbers 40
Multiplying by two-digit numbers 41
Multiplying three-digit by two-digit numbers 42
Review 43
Review 44
Special products 45

Division

Dividing 1-9 46
Divisors of 1, 7 .47
Divisors of 1, 6, 7 48
Divisors of 5, 6, 7 49
Divisors of 1, 7, 8 50
Divisors of 8, 9 .51
Division: Basic facts with remainders . . .52

Contents

One- and two-digit quotients with/without remainders 53
Dividing three-digit numbers 54
Zeros in quotients 55
Dividing by two-digit numbers 56
Dividing by two-digit numbers with remainders 57
Long division: two-digit dividend 58
Long division: three-digit dividend 59

Fractions and Decimals

Writing fractions 60
Writing fractions 61
Writing and shading fractions 62
Reducing fractions 63
Equivalent fractions 64
Improper fractions and mixed numbers 65
Comparing fractions 66
Adding and subtracting fractions with like denominators 67
Solving proportions 68
Relating decimals and fractions 69
Writing and comparing decimals 70
Adding and subtracting decimals; comparing decimals 71
Adding and subtracting decimals 72
Fractions and percentages 73

Measurement

Perimeter 74
Area 75
Volume 76
Temperature-Celsius, Fahrenheit 77

Shape

Quadrilaterals 78
Geometric shapes 79
Congruency; symmetry; circles 80
Congruence and similarity 81
Lines and angles 82
Measuring angles 83
Triangles 84

Data Handling

Charts 85
Line and bar graphs 86
Circle graphs; making graphs 87
Co-ordinates graph 88

Problem Solving

Addition facts 11-18 89
Two-digit subtraction 90
Comparisons 11-18 91
Cross-numerals puzzle 92
Dividing by two-and three-digit numbers 93
Critical thinking - make a million 94
Problem solving with fractions 95
Adding fractions with unlike denominators 96
Percentages 97
Faces, edges and vertices: Euler's Law 98

Millions and Millions

Name ______________________________

Skill: Place value - millions

Write each number in the place value boxes.

	Millions			Thousands			Ones		
1. 65,703,516		6							
2. 841,654,812									
3. 140,372,166									

Write the numbers.

4. five million, seven hundred thousand, nine hundred and two

   ___ , ___ ___ ___ , ___ ___ ___

5. 20,000,000 + 50,000 + 7,000 + 600 + 80 + 4

   ___ ___ , ___ ___ ___ , ___ ___ ___

6. one million, nine hundred and six thousand, two hundred and six

   ___ , ___ ___ ___ , ___ ___ ___

7. 2,000,000 + 600,000 + 40,000 + 300 + 20 + 1

   ___ , ___ ___ ___ , ___ ___ ___

8. nine million, two hundred and two thousand

   ___ , ___ ___ ___ , ___ ___ ___

9. twenty-five million, eight hundred and one

   ____

10. 19,000,000 + 50,000 + 900 + 5

    ____

11. 400,000,000 + 3,000,000 + 90,000 + 70 + 7

    ____

12. seventeen million, sixty-four thousand, and ninety-six

    ____

Big Fish

Name ______________________________

Skill: Place value - millions

Write the numbers in the puzzle.

Across

1. eight hundred and eighty-nine thousand, six hundred and twelve
6. forty-three thousand and eleven
8. eight thousand, four hundred and forty
9. three hundred million, eight hundred and sixty-five thousand, seven hundred and seventy-two
10. thirty-nine thousand and thirteen
11. six thousand, five hundred and eighty-eight
14. forty million, two thousand, one hundred and sixty-two
16. thirty thousand, one hundred and nine
18. five hundred and fifty thousand, one hundred and twenty-three
19. fifty thousand, seven hundred and eighty-six

Write the word name for each number.

Down

2. ______________________________
3. ______________________________
4. ______________________________
5. ______________________________
7. ______________________________
12. ______________________________
13. ______________________________
15. ______________________________
17. ______________________________

Let's Compare

Name ______________________________

Skill: Comparing numbers

Write > or <.

A.	10,769 ◯ 11,200	177,204 ◯ 116,791	97,213 ◯ 107,213
B.	86,190 ◯ 84,993	981,203 ◯ 918,203	72,218 ◯ 75,003
C.	198,221 ◯ 98,221	264,193 ◯ 266,001	83,103 ◯ 80,793
D.	656,183 ◯ 665,183	199,820 ◯ 198,993	55,186 ◯ 54,939

E. Write the numbers in order in the chart below.

756,802	694,213	820,000	971,246	378,461	192,874
471,622	216,606	92,813	87,214	63,744	55,806

Big	**Bigger**	**Biggest**
1.	5.	9.
2.	6.	10.
3.	7.	11.
4.	8.	12.

F. The smallest number is ______________.

The largest number is ______________.

G. Write the number that is 10 less than the smallest number. ______________

Write the number that is 100 more than the smallest number. ______________

Write the number that is 1000 more than the largest number. ______________

Round and Round

Name ______________________

Skill: Rounding numbers

Round each number to the nearest 10, 100 or 1000.

A. **10**	B. **100**	C. **1000**
85 ________	467 ________	5,764 ________
47 ________	821 ________	8,213 ________
293 ________	299 ________	9,621 ________
64 ________	1,371 ________	2,473 ________
327 ________	5,614 ________	1,121 ________

D. Round to the nearest thousand. Colour the balls when the numbers round up.

1. 4,651 ________
2. 9,961 ________
3. 7,208 ________
4. 2,976 ________
5. 899 ________
6. 3,479 ________
7. 6,411 ________
8. 5,743 ________
9. 1,372 ________
10. 4,493 ________
11. 7,510 ________
12. 6,821 ________
13. 2,093 ________
14. 4,499 ________
15. 8,803 ________

E. Answers for tens need to end in ______ zero(s).
Those for the nearest hundred end in ______ zero(s).
Answers to the nearest thousand end in ______ zero(s).

The Highest Peak

Name ______________________________

Skill: Highest common factor

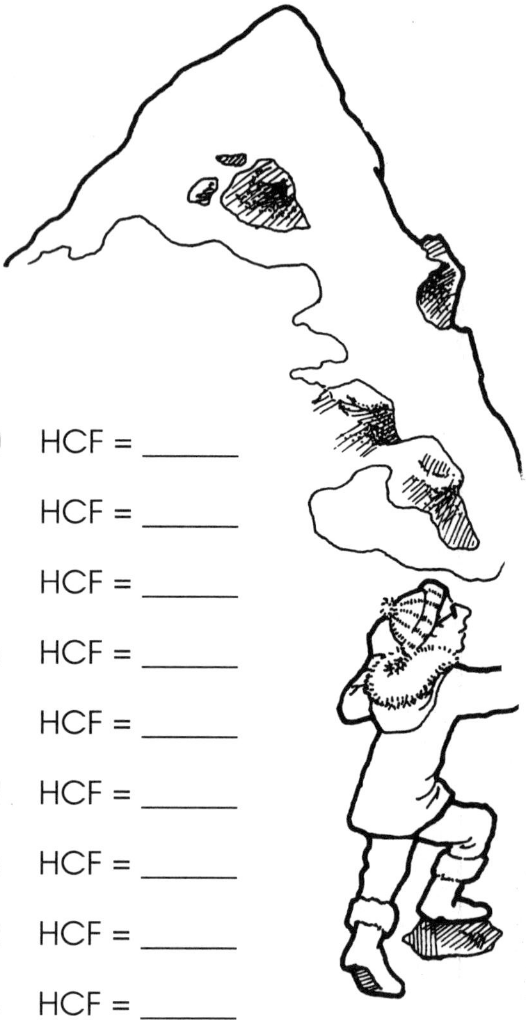

Find the highest common factor (HCF) for each pair of numbers. Then cross out one square at the bottom of the page that contains the answer. The letters to the remaining squares, written in order, will spell the answer to the following question:

What is the highest mountain peak in the world?

A.	12 and 30	HCF = ______	16 and 20	HCF = ______
B.	8 and 10	HCF = ______	7 and 9	HCF = ______
C.	6 and 12	HCF = ______	9 and 12	HCF = ______
D.	21 and 35	HCF = ______	10 and 16	HCF = ______
E.	12 and 18	HCF = ______	14 and 21	HCF = ______
F.	15 and 40	HCF = ______	36 and 48	HCF = ______
G.	16 and 24	HCF = ______	18 and 36	HCF = ______
H.	21 and 45	HCF = ______	24 and 42	HCF = ______
I.	18 and 30	HCF = ______	45 and 54	HCF = ______
J.	22 and 52	HCF = ______	16 and 64	HCF = ______

M 0	A 4	C 6	O 30	J 5	H 2	U 11	L 12
P 6	N 15	Q 3	B 7	T 10	H 6	Y 8	E 13
Z 18	U 7	V 22	G 3	X 1	E 20	R 14	K 6
F 2	E 17	W 6	S 21	C 9	J 2	D 16	T 25

___ ___ ___ ___ ___   ___ ___ ___ ___ ___ ___ ___

"Just About" Answers

Name ______________________________

Skill: Estimating sums and differences

Use rounding to estimate each sum or difference below. Then shade a section in the box at the bottom of the page that matches your answer to find a secret word.

A. $28 + 92 = 120$ $73 + 68$ $133 - 67$ $166 - 78$ $617 + 376$

B. $44 + 59$ $1{,}486 - 626$ $681 - 324$ $6{,}790 + 3{,}456$ $15{,}897 - 8{,}584$

C. $368 + 429$ $1{,}295 - 787$ $1{,}869 - 451$ $1{,}303 - 698$ $17{,}498 - 8{,}329$

D. $12{,}645 - 9{,}103$ $698 - 462$ $2{,}375 + 2{,}814$ $1{,}014 + 5{,}321$ $8{,}247 + 9{,}983$

120	7,000	400	3,000	1,000	19,000	
4,000	300	140	8,000	1,400	9,000	15,000
800	700	5,000	11,000	18,000	14,000	17,000
200	2,000	90	12,000	6,000	10,000	20,000
600	60	500	16,000	100	13,000	900

What's the secret word? ______________

"Sum Difference"

Skill: Estimating sums and differences

Name ______________________________

Estimate each sum or difference by rounding each number to the nearest hundred. Add or subtract. Shade in the boxes that have answers of 500 or more.

1. 927 − 419 (900 − 400)	2. 841 + 219	3. 164 + 99	4. 617 − 302
5. 897 − 143	6. 222 + 170	7. 719 − 504	8. 921 − 647
9. 302 + 256	10. 392 + 184	11. 621 − 304	12. 640 + 599
13. 163 + 173	14. 610 − 601	15. 707 − 290	16. 701 + 291
17. 816 + 219	18. 999 − 702	19. 797 − 142	20. 146 + 208
21. 504 − 392	22. 109 + 99	23. 697 − 64	24. 299 − 199

Another Kind of Number

Name ______________________________ Skill: Roman numerals

A. Finish the chart.

I = 1	VII = ____	XL = 40	C = 100	DC = 600
II = 2	VIII = ____	L = 50	CC = _____	DCC = 700
III = 3	IX = 9	LX = 60	CCC = _____	DCCL = _____
IV = 4	X = 10	LXX = ____	CCCL = _____	DCCC = _____
V = ____	XX = ____	LXXX = ____	CD = 400	CM = 900
VI = 6	XXX = ____	XC = 90	D = _____	M = 1,000

B. To make the numbers between 10–13, add ones (I) to ten (X).

Write 11, 12, and 13 in Roman numerals. 11 = ______ 12 = ______ 13 = ______

Fifteen is 10 + 5, or ______.

For 16, 17, and 18, add ones to 15. 16 = ______ 17 = ______ 18 = ______

For 14, subtract 1 from 15 by putting the one in front of 5. 14 = ______

For 19, subtract 1 from 20 by putting the one in front of the second 10. 19 = ______

C. Following the rules above, write the numbers.

XXII = ______ XXXIII = ______ LII = ______ CDXCI = ______

CL = ______ CLX = ______ DL = ______ DCLI = ______

D. Draw lines to match.

CCCX	560	XVI	24
XXXIV	8	CCXC	16
DLX	310	DX	19
VIII	34	XIX	290
XIV	805	XXIV	510
DCCCV	14	MMCIX	740
MIX	1,009	DCCXL	2,109

Riddle

Skill: 2-and 3-digit addends, regrouping

Name ______________________________

Riddle: The answer is a walkie-talkie.

___ ___ ___ ___   ___ ___   ___ ___ u
511 455 534 850   163 954   886 954

___ ___ ___   ___ ___ ___ ___   ___ ___ u
660 730 850   511 455 730 571   886 954

___ ___ ___ ___ ___   ___
843 838 954 980 980   534

___ ___ ___ ___ ___ ___ ___ ___ ___
843 730 571 850 973 397 730 163 730

___ ___ ___ ___   ___   ___ ___ ___ ___ ___?
511 973 850 455   534   838 534 163 973 954

A 418 + 116	**C** 724 + 119	**D** 128 + 35	**E** 414 + 316	**G** 25 + 635
H 39 + 416	**I** 349 + 624	**N** 524 + 47	**O** 427 + 527	**P** 289 + 108
R 519 + 319	**S** 127 + 853	**T** 811 + 39	**W** 28 + 483	**Y** 327 + 559

A Happy Thought

Skill: 2-and 3-digit addends, regrouping

Name ______________________________

___ ___ ___ ___ ___   ___ ___   ___ ___ ___
858 576 973 973 442   634 442   150 973 973

___ ___ ___   ___ ___ ___ ___ ___ ___ ___
634 858 576   662 790 371 576 357 83 732

___ ' ___ ___   ___ ___ ___   ___ ___
371 638 576   972 576 634   634 442

___ ___ ___ ___ !
64 576 576 634

A 113 + 37	**D** 46 + 37	**E** 529 + 47	**F** 18 + 644	**H** 29 + 829
I 126 + 245	**L** 427 + 546	**M** 29 + 35	**N** 109 + 248	**O** 228 + 214
R 447 + 343	**S** 416 + 316	**T** 419 + 215	**V** 219 + 419	**Y** 143 + 829

Tongue Twister

Skill: 2-and 3-digit addends, regrouping

Name ______________________________

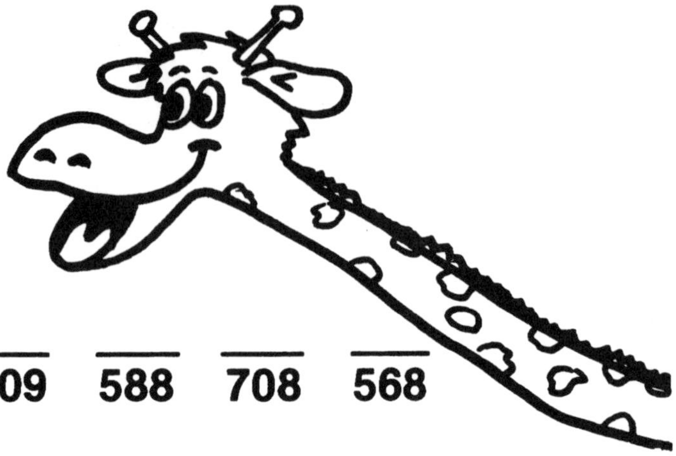

___ ___ ___ ___ ___ ___ ___ ___
924 647 450 406 609 588 708 568

___ ___ ___ ___ ___ ___ ___ ___
924 616 647 450 588 588 609 938

___ ___ ___ ___ ___   ___ ___
924 647 450 306 609   576 227

___ ___ ___ ___ ___ ___ ___ ___
924 616 924 450 227 840 616 406

___ ___ ___ ___ ___ ___ .
924 647 450 829 609 938

A 260 + 190	**C** 150 + 256	**E** 532 + 77	**F** 397 + 191	**G** 462 + 462
I 240 + 376	**L** 287 + 281	**N** 173 + 54	**O** 386 + 190	**P** 648 + 181
R 573 + 74	**S** 767 + 171	**T** 450 + 390	**U** 346 + 362	**Z** 113 + 193

A Tongue Twister

Name ______________________

Skill: 3-digit addends, no regrouping

___ ___ ___ ___ ___   ___ ___ ___ ___ ___ ___
698 587 339 587 739   698 949 483 339 587 509

___ ___ ___ ___ ___ ___
698 739 357 799 587 698

___ ___ ___ ___ ___ ___ ___ ___ ___
698 483 949 228 448 587 509 587 444

___ ___ ___ ___ ___ y
698 483 299 593 483

___ ___ ___ ___ ___ ___ ___ ___ ___ .
698 299 559 228 448 593 357 509 444

A 234 + 123	D 221 + 223	E 233 + 354	H 320 + 128	I 713 + 236
K 308 + 491	L 300 + 183	N 524 + 215	O 128 + 171	R 406 + 103
S 495 + 203	T 125 + 103	U 328 + 231	V 216 + 123	W 272 + 321

A Tongue Twister

Skill: 3-digit addends, regrouping

Name ______________________________

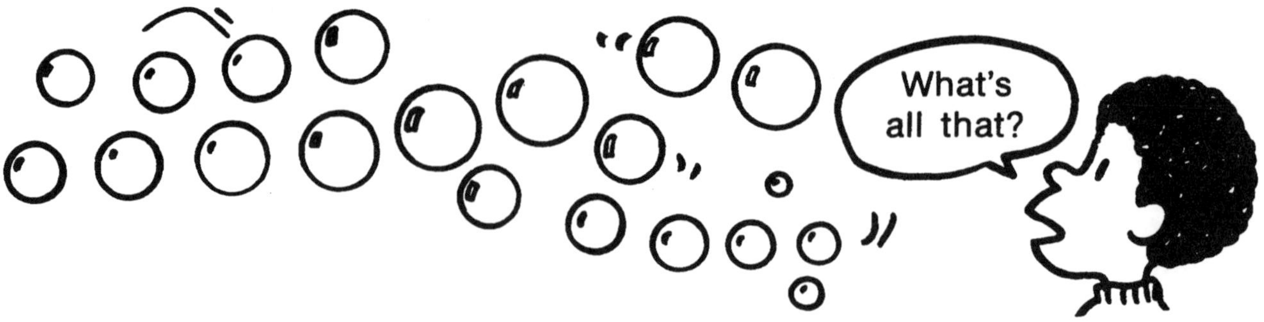

___ 652   ___ 890 ___ 666 ___ 593 ___ 785 ___ 950 ___ 793   ___ 890 ___ 394 ___ 212 ___ 371

___ 890 ___ 666 ___ 991 ___ 874 ___ 793 ___ 991 ___ 442 ___ 652 ___ 212 ___ 666 ___ 212 ___ 442

___ 890 ___ 394 ___ 371 ___ 910   ___ 890 ___ 593 ___ 394 ___ 394 ___ 593 ___ 991 ___ 874 ___ 442

___ 991 ___ 668   ___ 890 ___ 666 ___ 991 ___ 910 ___ 874

___ 890 ___ 212 ___ 890 ___ 890 ___ 394 ___ 371 ___ 442 .

A 436 + 216	**B** 771 + 119	**E** 157 + 214	**F** 529 + 139	**G** 358 + 427
H 845 + 105	**I** 164 + 429	**L** 207 + 187	**N** 525 + 349	**O** 185 + 806
R 538 + 128	**S** 223 + 219	**T** 558 + 235	**U** 109 + 103	**W** 705 + 205

A Riddle

Skill: 3-digit addends, regrouping

Name ______________________________

Riddle: Why do monsters forget?

___ ___ ___ ___ ___ ___ ___ ___ ___ ___
929 612 929 944 534 627 695 988 934 867

___ ___ ___ ___   ___ ___   ___ ___ ___
867 504 929 643   988 934   504 934 929

___ ___ ___   ___ ___ ___
929 807 944   807 934 339

___ ___ ___   ___ ___ ___
504 510 627   627 695 929

___ ___ ___ ___ ___   ___ ___ ___.
504 627 695 929 944   643 988 745

A 343 + 464	**D** 166 + 173	**E** 299 + 630	**G** 585 + 282	**H** 541 + 154
I 293 + 695	**N** 583 + 351	**O** 292 + 212	**R** 793 + 151	**S** 350 + 293
T 493 + 134	**U** 130 + 380	**V** 351 + 261	**X** 453 + 292	**Y** 343 + 191

Adding Larger Numbers

Name ______________________

Skill: 4-digit addition

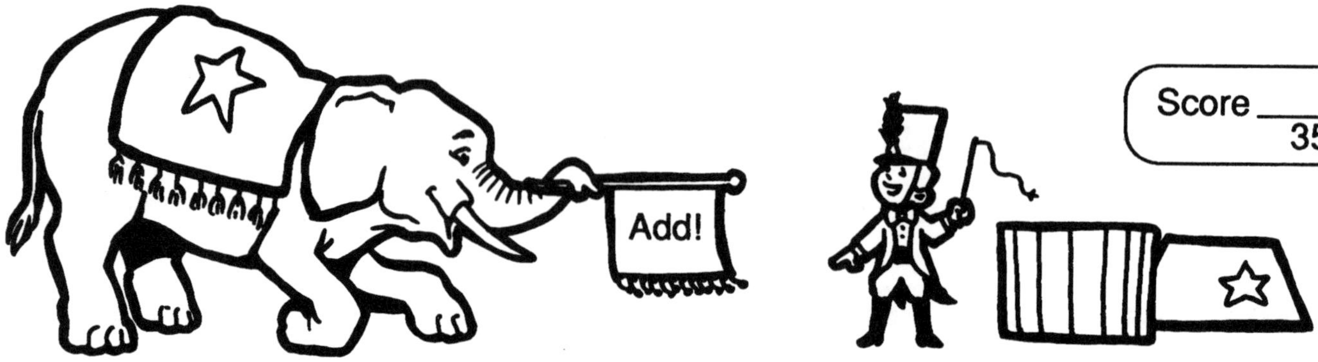

Score ____ / 35

A.	2,714 + 3,281	4,265 + 5,135	6,223 + 290	2,227 + 1,462	5,540 + 1,628
B.	4,175 + 377	1,097 + 1,983	7,142 + 2,355	8,426 + 722	1,014 + 792
C.	6,514 + 1,922	3,555 + 1,671	892 + 3,419	5,001 + 4,232	1,660 + 2,237
D.	1,554 + 667	8,817 + 1,012	5,572 + 918	1,090 + 703	2,813 + 2,763
E.	4,272 + 624	1,456 + 1,417	5,915 + 1,775	1,500 + 1,458	7,254 + 746
F.	2,754 + 2,787	2,861 + 668	7,565 + 1,907	4,841 + 1,827	5,817 + 2,062
G.	1,533 + 1,316	2,376 + 1,849	4,458 + 998	8,814 + 1,092	3,464 + 3,721

Shapely Sums

Skill: 4-digit addition

Name ______________________________

Working diagonally, add the numbers shown by the arrows.
Write >, <, or = to compare the sums.

1.

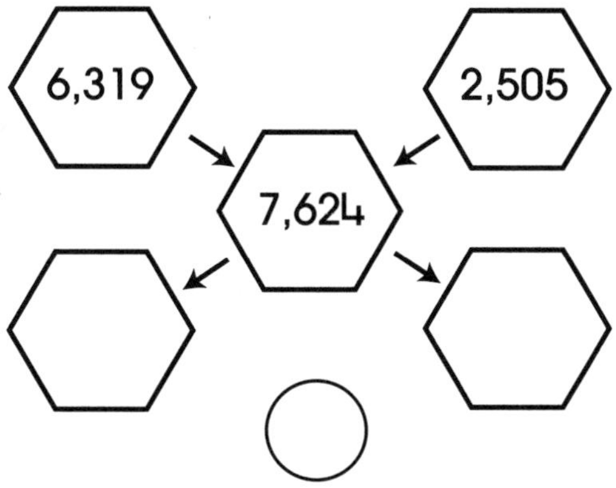

2.

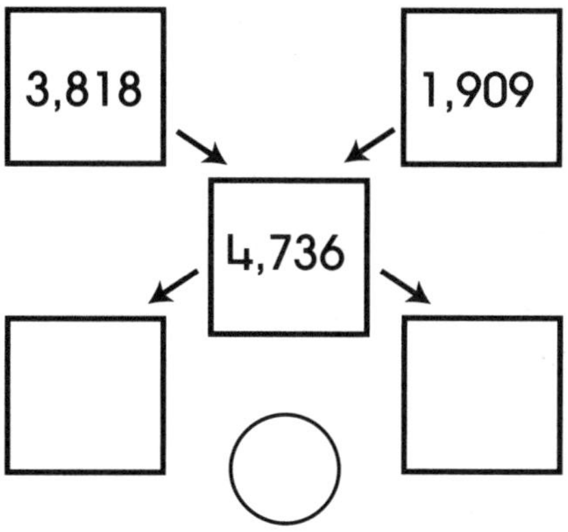

3.

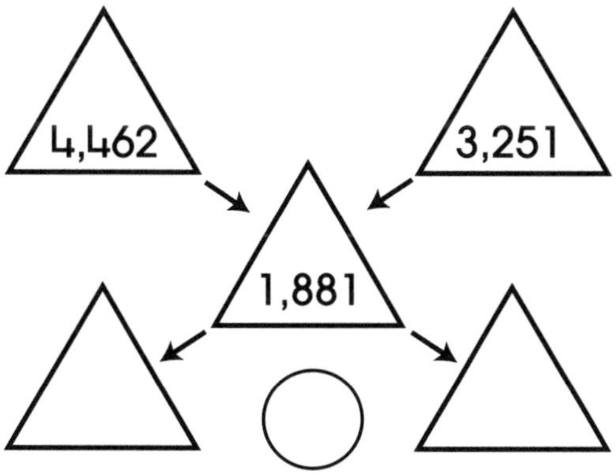

4.

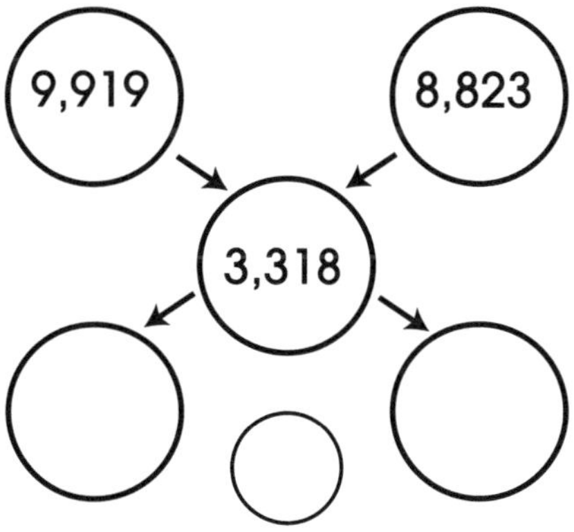

5.

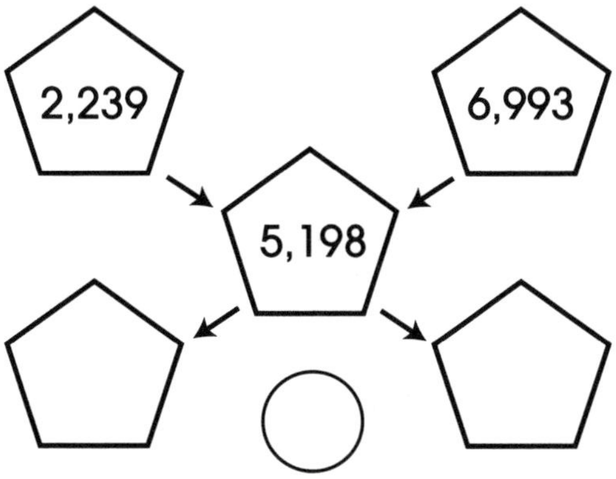

6.

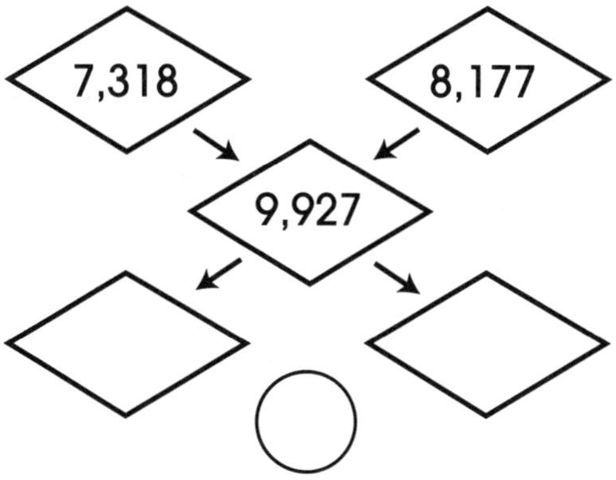

Write the name of the shape in each puzzle.

1. ____________ 2. ____________ 3. ____________

4. ____________ 5. ____________ 6. ____________

Flower Problems

Skill: Subtracting multiples of 10

Name ______________________

Score ____ / 40

Write the answers in the petals.

Brainwork! Now create your own flower problem. Put 100 or 190 in the centre.

Taking a Bite

Skill: 2-digit subtraction, regrouping

Name ______________________

Score ____ / 35

Subtract and write the answers. To find where the worm bit the apple, colour the box with the greatest answer.

A.		24 − 13	86 − 52	89 − 36	77 − 5	
B.	57 − 22	19 − 5	68 − 24	71 − 50	86 − 13	50 − 10
C.	69 − 23	88 − 12	45 − 13	28 − 12	94 − 24	76 − 73
D.	52 − 10	79 − 61	49 − 22	70 − 40	95 − 4	87 − 12
E.	79 − 70	39 − 11	36 − 32	28 − 2	99 − 55	98 − 15
F.		77 − 45	68 − 20	49 − 32	87 − 30	
G.		88 − 72	76 − 21	99 − 68		

Space Walk

Skill: 2-digit subtraction, regrouping

Name ________________________________

34 — Yellow
35 — Orange
36 — Brown
37 — Blue

Colour all the spaces and boxes.

72 - 37	66 - 29	82 - 45	94 - 57	54 - 17	63 - 27	75 - 38	56 - 19
90 - 55	74 - 37	82 - 48	84 - 47	64 - 28	74 - 38	93 - 57	66 - 29
52 - 17	93 - 56	52 - 15	74 - 37	95 - 58	83 - 47	55 - 18	63 - 26
62 - 27	95 - 58	73 - 39	54 - 17	76 - 39	94 - 58	53 - 16	86 - 49
71 - 36	50 - 13	62 - 28	83 - 46	64 - 27	70 - 34	84 - 47	65 - 28

Number Books

Skill: 2-digit subtraction, regrouping

Name ______________________________

Colour all the spaces and boxes.

16 — Red
17 — Orange
18 — Yellow

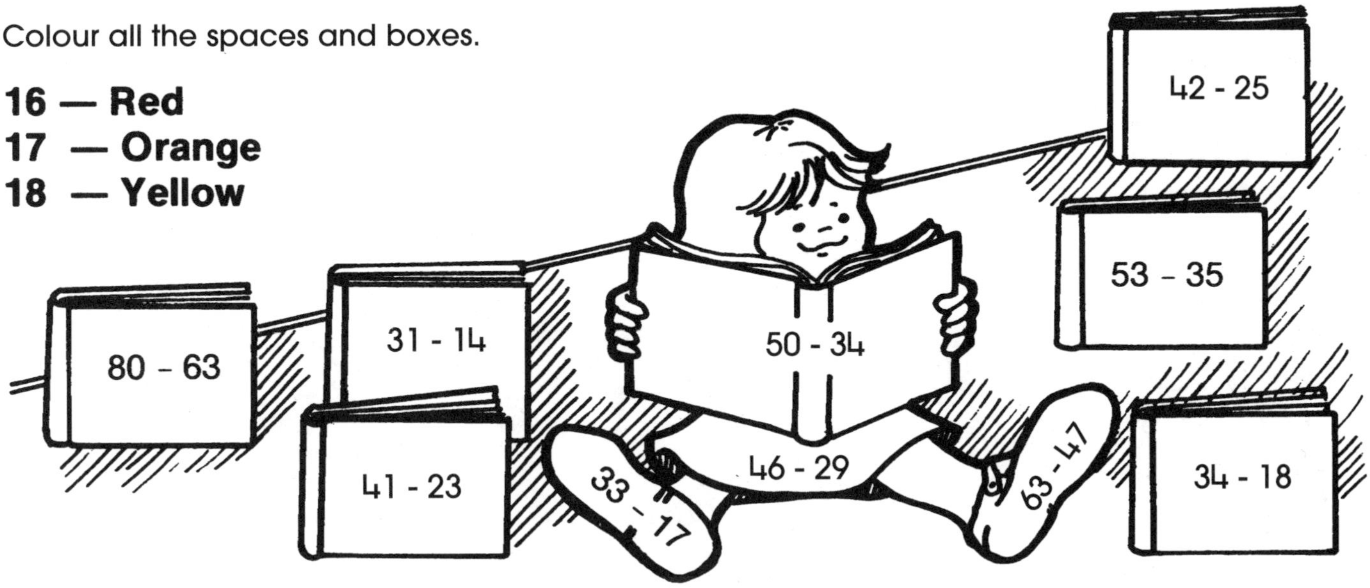

95 − 79	45 − 29	70 − 54	65 − 49	32 − 14	94 − 76	54 − 36	84 − 66
91 − 75	42 − 24	71 − 53	57 − 39	72 − 54	91 − 73	35 − 17	92 − 74
51 − 35	42 − 24	82 − 66	55 − 39	93 − 75	60 − 43	71 − 54	95 − 78
83 − 67	45 − 27	54 − 36	95 − 79	44 − 26	62 − 45	77 − 59	90 − 73
61 − 45	83 − 67	41 − 25	80 − 64	93 − 75	74 − 57	40 − 23	75 − 58

Counting frogs

Skill: 2-digit subtraction, regrouping

Name ____________________________

34 — Red
35 — Blue
36 — Brown
37 — Green

Colour all the spaces and boxes.

72 - 38	80 - 45	52 - 17	54 - 19	84 - 49	63 - 28	50 - 13	70 - 35
53 - 19	90 - 55	51 - 16	92 - 57	50 - 15	85 - 48	63 - 26	96 - 59
60 - 26	82 - 47	82 - 46	65 - 29	62 - 26	93 - 58	83 - 46	61 - 26
83 - 49	71 - 36	62 - 26	81 - 46	73 - 37	53 - 18	71 - 34	62 - 27
92 - 58	83 - 48	71 - 35	85 - 49	84 - 48	64 - 29	51 - 14	74 - 39

Crowing For Corn

Skill: 3-digit subtraction, regrouping

Name ______________________________

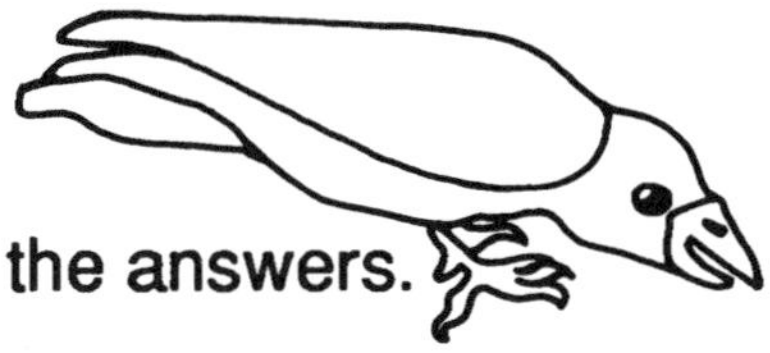

Score ____
35

Write the answers.

A.	B.	C.	D.	E.
594 − 306	862 − 615	426 − 108	990 − 509	748 − 129
771 − 226	413 − 308	980 − 313	662 − 327	965 − 217
891 − 443	747 − 209	344 − 237	630 − 403	863 − 537
884 − 349	268 − 29	671 − 524	690 − 177	564 − 46
292 − 139	583 − 165	892 − 258	365 − 108	590 − 115
970 − 236	780 − 114	795 − 529	571 − 455	645 − 328
745 − 416	577 − 208	593 − 389	983 − 276	751 − 129

Brainwork! Circle one of the problems above. Write a word problem to go with it.

Subtraction Balancing Act

Name ______________________________

Skill: 3-digit subtraction, regrouping

Score ____ / 35

Subtract and write the answers.

A.	737 − 450	956 − 895	638 − 147	968 − 486	928 − 345	526 − 336
B.	627 − 282	919 − 622	958 − 262	959 − 571	829 − 179	419 − 350
C.	814 − 362	628 − 390	375 − 193	837 − 762	637 − 481	847 − 464
D.	946 − 794	748 − 273	849 − 254	727 − 465	768 − 674	829 − 558
E.	768 − 398	989 − 197	478 − 181	619 − 546	437 − 296	847 − 683
F.	437 − 77	759 − 585	672 − 280	549 − 183	876 − 283	

Brainwork! Write a subtraction word problem about a circus seal. Solve the problem.

Funny Frog

Skill: 3-digit subtraction, regrouping

Name ______________________________

Score ____
25

First subtract and write the answers. Then use the key to write a letter below each problem. Read the riddle and its answer.

522 − 246	881 − 93	550 − 174	721 − 196
W			

943 − 278	842 − 186

851 − 587	617 − 259	955 − 299	488 − 199	782 − 296

188	=	N
264	=	F
276	=	W
289	=	G
358	=	R
376	=	A
454	=	I
477	=	E
486	=	S
525	=	T
585	=	P
599	=	K
656	=	O
665	=	D
788	=	H

851 − 587	656 − 298	829 − 375	666 − 478	797 − 198

741 − 365	897 − 372

754 − 169	944 − 568	794 − 436	703 − 178	723 − 269	802 − 325	609 − 123

Answer: CROAKA-COLA!

Brainwork! Write subtraction problems and a matching key to spell out a name for the frog. Ask a friend to solve your puzzle.

Cat and Mouse Maze

Skill: 3-digit subtraction, with/without regrouping

Name ______________________________

Score ____ / 40

Help mouse run to a hole before Cat wakes up. Subtract and write the answers. Then begin at the START and colour all the boxes with answers that are even numbers.

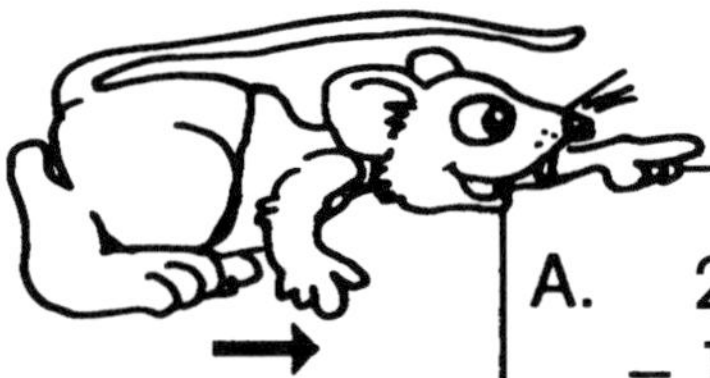

→ START

START	A. 289 − 143	856 − 198	707 − 158	857 − 812	709 − 102
B. 645 − 272	932 − 285	302 − 146	682 − 381	529 − 120	685 − 192
C. 749 − 334	456 − 109	582 − 498	838 − 770	511 − 165	999 − 283
D. 566 − 233	889 − 266	631 − 328	458 − 291	953 − 776	804 − 128
E. 880 − 449	787 − 184	628 − 493	489 − 72	809 − 139	458 − 228
F. 250 − 89	179 − 126	581 − 126	818 − 191	832 − 678	501 − 178
G. 493 − 256	357 − 108	701 − 204	510 − 99	849 − 101	

Brainwork! Write a word problem to match one of the problems above.

Zeros Are Important

Name ______________________________

Skill: 2 to 5-digit subtraction

A. Subtract. Add to check your answers.

1. 207 − 143 = 64 (check: 64 + 143 = 207)

2. 100 − 64 = ____ + ____

3. 602 − 314 = ____ + ____

4. 5,007 − 2,106 = ____ + ____

5. 4,109 − 1,174 = ____ + ____

6. 3,000 − 2,674 = ____ + ____

7. 9,008 − 3,962 = ____ + ____

8. 12,003 − 10,666 = ____ + ____

9. 70,405 − 21,510 = ____ + ____

B. Write the problems below in column form and subtract.
Write the answers in correct order from smallest to largest.

1. 560 − 392 = ________
2. 4,300 − 571 = ________
3. 5,000 − 297 = ________
4. 640 − 399 = ________
5. 7,040 − 2,607 = ________
6. 1,007 − 352 = ________

largest

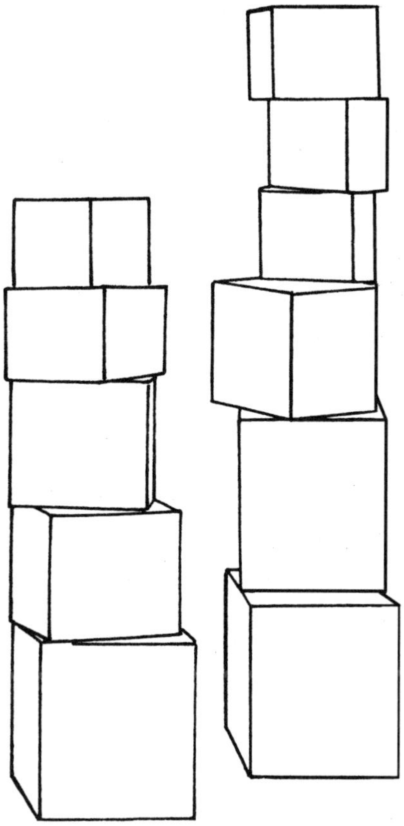

smallest

1. ________ 2. ________ 3. ________ 4. ________ 5. ________ 6. ________

Working with Numbers

Skill: 4-Digit subtraction

Name ______________________________

8795 − 3452	9688 − 2057
7640 − 2605	6839 − 2479
8230 − 7519	
5761 − 4299	8596 − 2348
6057 − 1808	3085 − 1507
4306 − 1552	9205 − 4621
8621 − 5934	7413 − 3895

Keep on track

Skill: Addition and subtraction: 3 and 4 - digit numbers

Name ____________________________

Begin the race and continue on the track. Add or subtract the amounts shown in the key.

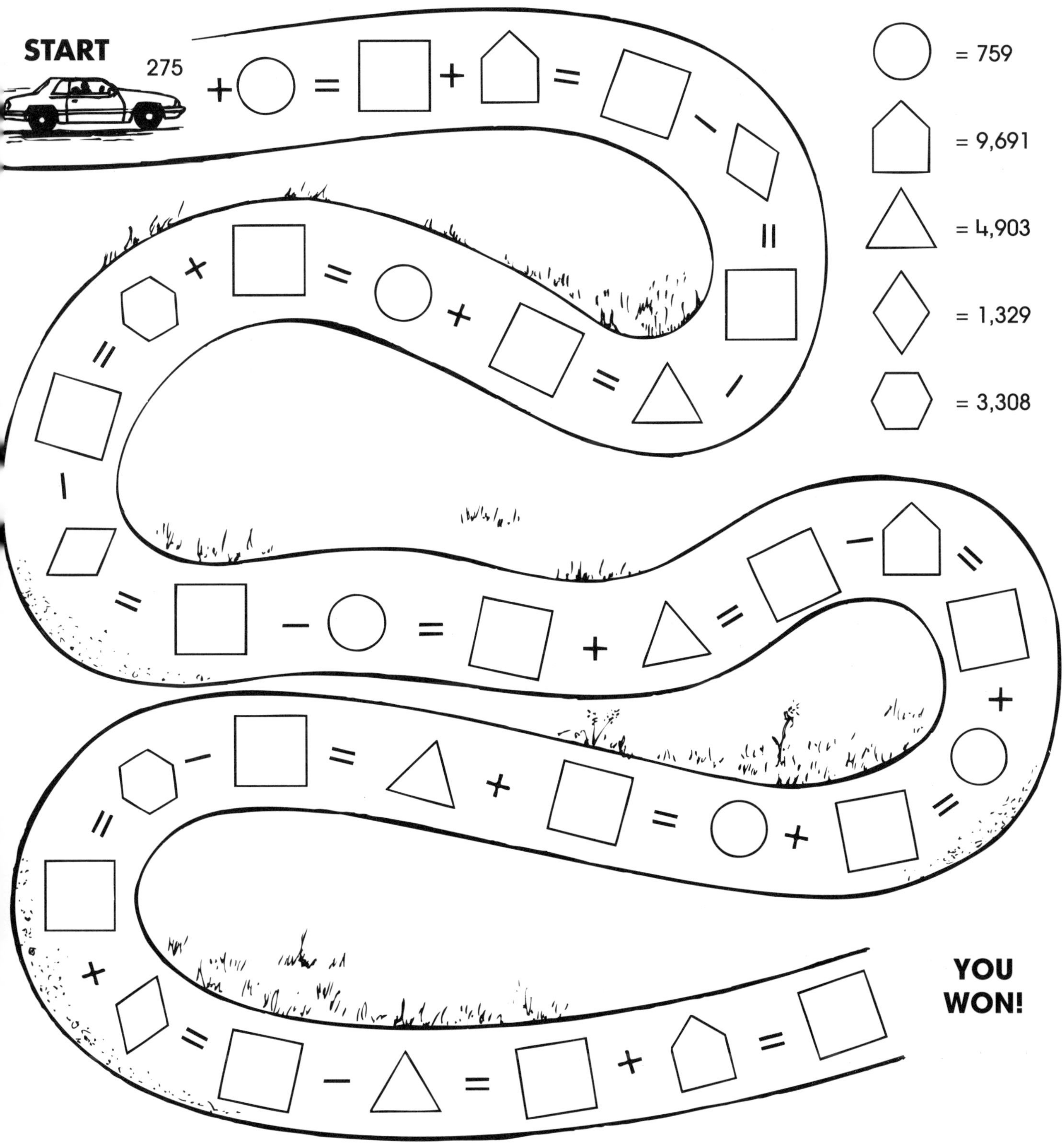

Talk With the Animals

Name ______________________________

Skill: Adding and subtracting 3, 4 and 5-digit numbers

Add or subtract. Use your answers to write and solve a riddle.

O. 5,038 + 2,847

W. 6,034 − 2,993

N. 7,645 + 8,397

C. 57,634 + 18,906

D. 9,634 − 5,798

E. 3,497 + 867

K. 4,263 − 1,896

H. 9,156 + 8,375

P. 54,375 − 36,693

L. 3,073 − 897

U. 5,372 − 439

A. 23,842 − 1,632

S. 32,693 + 41,221

I. 14,734 − 2,961

F. 1,646 + 1,826 = ______ G. 9,874 − 8,887 = ______ T. 4,419 + 2,987 = ______

___ ___ ___ ___ ___ ___ ___ ___ ___
3,041 17,531 22,210 7,406 3,836 7,885 4,364 73,914 22,210

___ ___ ___ ___ ___ ___ ___ ___ ___ ___ ___ ___
76,540 17,531 11,773 76,540 2,367 4,364 16,042 73,914 17,682 4,364 22,210 2,367 **?**

___ ___ ___ ___ ___ ___ ___ ___ ___ ___ ___ ___
3,472 7,885 3,041 2,176 2,176 22,210 16,042 987 4,993 22,210 987 4,364

Tracking Down Facts?

Name ______________________

Skill: Multiplication facts, 0-9 as factors

Write the missing factor or product.

A.
6 x ___ = 30
8 x 4 = ___
___ x 3 = 21
9 x ___ = 81
0 x 4 = ___
9 x 3 = ___
6 x ___ = 12
4 x 4 = ___
___ x 5 = 40
3 x ___ = 9

B.
3 x 8 = ___
5 x 4 = ___
___ x 3 = 0
8 x ___ = 8
2 x 7 = ___
___ x 5 = 25
6 x ___ = 54
6 x 4 = ___
7 x ___ = 42
3 x ___ = 12

C.
2 x 5 = ___
___ x 7 = 49
3 x ___ = 15
8 x 2 = ___
___ x 6 = 36
9 x ___ = 63
___ x 9 = 45
___ x 2 = 4
1 x 0 = ___
3 x 6 = ___

D.
2 x 4 = ___
___ x 7 = 7
6 x ___ = 48
8 x 5 = ___
___ x 1 = 3
5 x ___ = 35
___ x 9 = 72
___ x 2 = 6
7 x ___ = 28
8 x 8 = ___

E.
___ x 4 = 36
5 x ___ = 30
___ x 7 = 7
1 x ___ = 5
0 x 6 = ___
___ x 1 = 1
4 x ___ = 36
___ x 9 = 18
___ x 2 = 0
7 x 8 = ___

Score
___
50

Brainwork! Write four multiplication problems that have 7 as a missing factor.

Beat the Clock!

Skill: Multiplication facts, 0-10 as factors

Name ___________________________

A. Complete this chart by multiplying.

Example:

X	1	2
1	1	2
2	2	4

Can you finish it in five minutes or less?

Score ____ / 100

X	1	2	3	4	5	6	7	8	9	10
1										
2										
3										
4										
5										
6										
7										
8										
9										
10										

X	7	1	5	2	6	9	3	8	0	4
4										
9										
6										
1										
5										
8										
0										
3										
7										
2										

B. This multiplication chart is a little harder because the numbers are out of order.

Can you finish it in eight minutes or less?

Score ____ / 100

Multiplying All Around

Name ____________________

Skill: Multiplying 1-9 as factors

Multiply the centre numbers by the numbers in the middle rings.

1.

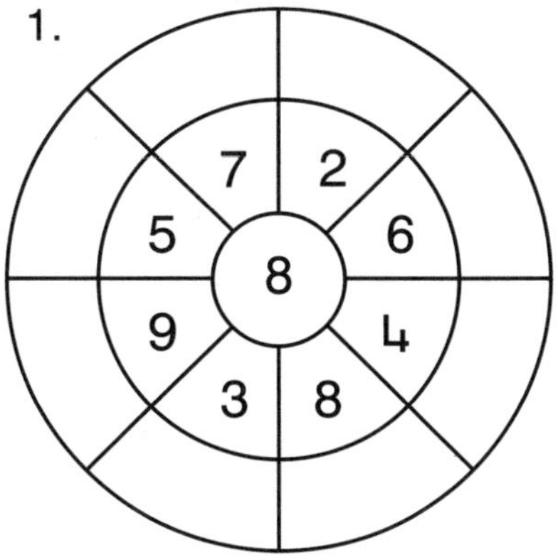

2.

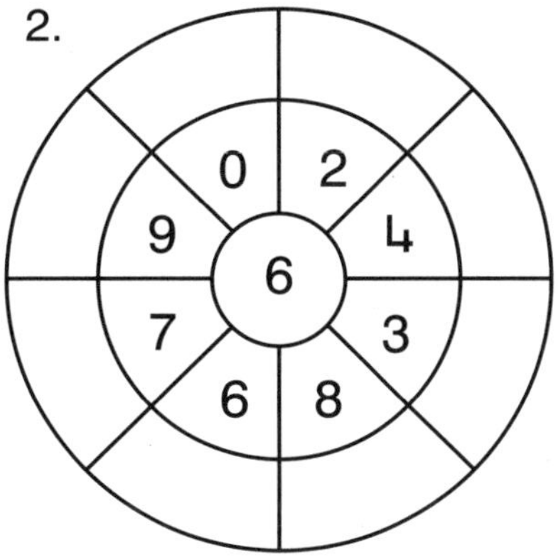

3.

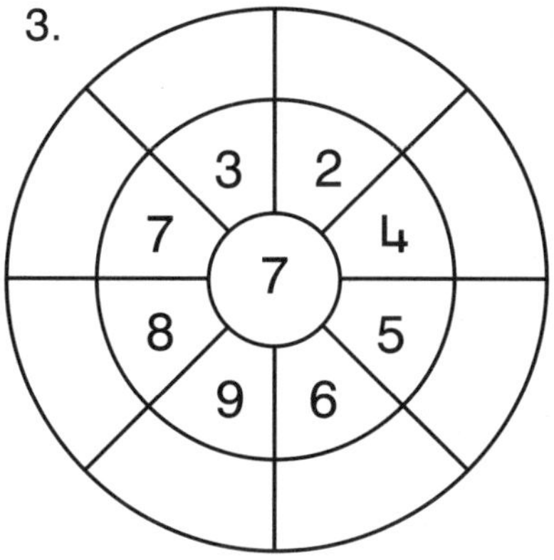

4.

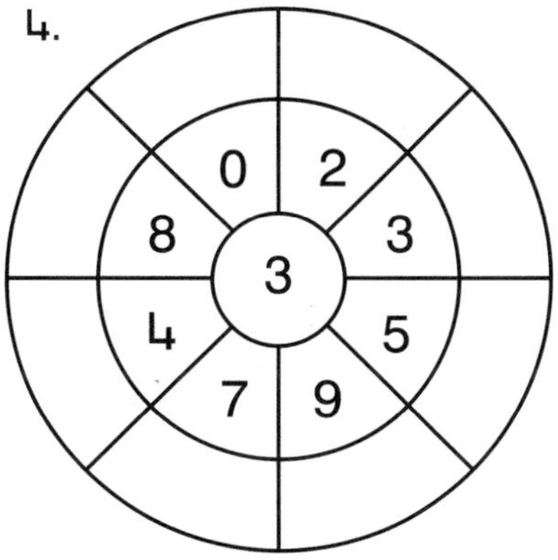

5.

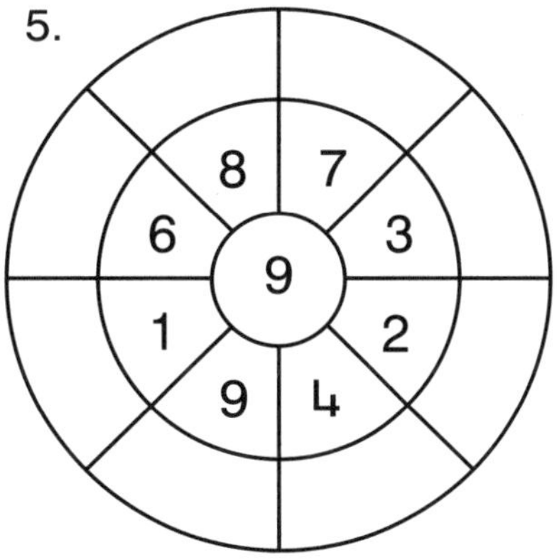

6.

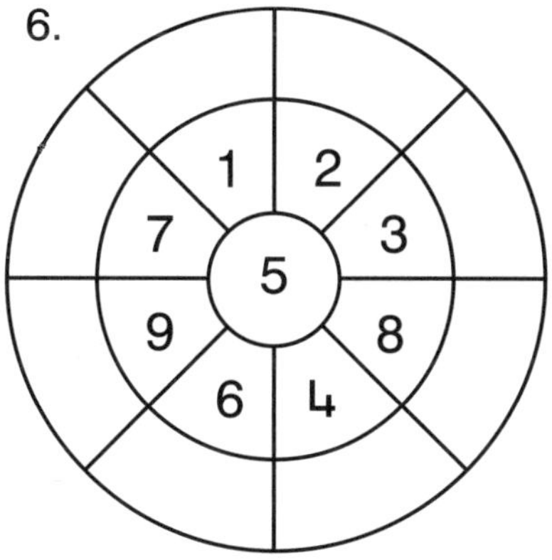

7.

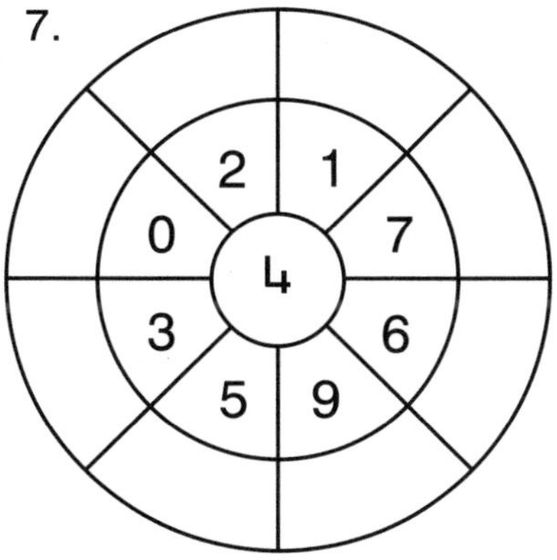

8.

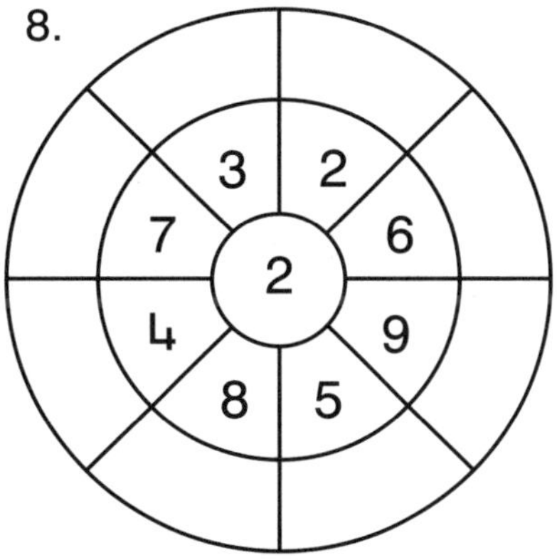

9.

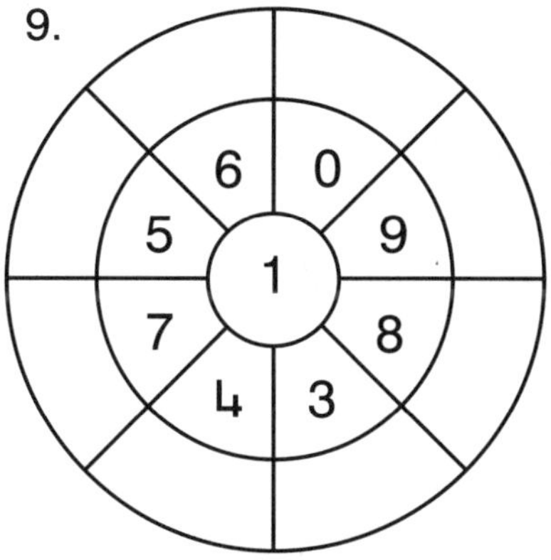

Know-It-All Knights

Skill: Multiplying by 5 and 6

Name ______________________

Write each product. Cross off the answer on the matching shield.

A. 4 x 5 = ____

3 x 5 = ____

8 x 5 = ____

7 x 5 = ____

0 x 5 = ____

9 x 5 = ____

5 x 5 = ____

1 x 5 = ____

6 x 5 = ____

2 x 5 = ____

B. 3 x 6 = ____

1 x 6 = ____

6 x 6 = ____

5 x 6 = ____

9 x 6 = ____

0 x 6 = ____

7 x 6 = ____

2 x 6 = ____

8 x 6 = ____

4 x 6 = ____

Solve each problem.

C. 6 x 7	**D.** 5 x 8	**E.** 5 x 3	**F.** 6 x 4	**G.** 5 x 7	**H.** 6 x 5
I. 6 x 6	**J.** 6 x 0	**K.** 5 x 5	**L.** 6 x 9	**M.** 5 x 9	**N.** 5 x 1
O. 5 x 4	**P.** 6 x 8	**Q.** 5 x 7	**R.** 6 x 2		Score ____ / 36

Brainwork! If a number is multiplied by 5, the answer will always end in one of two numbers. Write the two numbers.

Kangaroo Fun

Name ______________________

Skill: Multiplying by 5, 6, 7, 8 and 9

Multiply and write the answers.

A.

3 x 7 = ____
5 x 9 = ____
0 x 6 = ____
4 x 5 = ____
1 x 8 = ____
9 x 7 = ____
3 x 6 = ____
2 x 8 = ____
8 x 5 = ____
4 x 9 = ____

B.

6 x 8 = ____
8 x 9 = ____
5 x 6 = ____
1 x 5 = ____
4 x 7 = ____
0 x 9 = ____
8 x 6 = ____
3 x 5 = ____
7 x 7 = ____
9 x 8 = ____

C.

5 x 5 = ____
6 x 6 = ____
2 x 7 = ____
0 x 8 = ____
3 x 9 = ____
7 x 5 = ____
1 x 9 = ____
4 x 8 = ____
9 x 6 = ____
6 x 7 = ____

D.

7 x 6 = ____
0 x 5 = ____
9 x 9 = ____
1 x 7 = ____
3 x 8 = ____
7 x 9 = ____
2 x 5 = ____
8 x 7 = ____
5 x 8 = ____
2 x 6 = ____

E.

1 x 6 = ____
7 x 8 = ____
6 x 5 = ____
6 x 9 = ____
5 x 7 = ____
9 x 5 = ____
2 x 9 = ____
4 x 6 = ____
8 x 8 = ____
0 x 7 = ____

Brainwork! Write a word problem about kangaroos that can be solved using a multiplication fact from this page.

Skydiving

Skill: Multiplying by 7 and 8

Name ______________________________

Write each product. Cross off the answer on the matching parachute.

A. 4 x 7 = ____

7 x 7 = ____

1 x 7 = ____

3 x 7 = ____

5 x 7 = ____

6 x 7 = ____

0 x 7 = ____

2 x 7 = ____

9 x 7 = ____

8 x 7 = ____

B. 8 x 8 = ____

3 x 8 = ____

0 x 8 = ____

7 x 8 = ____

4 x 8 = ____

1 x 8 = ____

6 x 8 = ____

9 x 8 = ____

2 x 8 = ____

5 x 8 = ____

Solve each problem.

C. 8 x 6	**D.** 7 x 1	**E.** 7 x 5	**F.** 8 x 4	**G.** 7 x 7	**H.** 8 x 8
I. 8 x 5	**J.** 8 x 0	**K.** 7 x 9	**L.** 8 x 3	**M.** 8 x 9	**N.** 7 x 2
O. 7 x 3	**P.** 7 x 8	**Q.** 8 x 2	**R.** 7 x 6	 Score ____ / 36	

Brainwork! Write a word problem that can be solved using this fact: 7 x 8 = 56

A Bright Bouquet

Name ______________________

Skill: Multiplying by 9 and 10

Write each product. Cross off the answer on the matching flowers.

A. 2 x 9 = ____

9 x 9 = ____

0 x 9 = ____

3 x 9 = ____

4 x 9 = ____

10 x 9 = ____

7 x 9 = ____

1 x 9 = ____

5 x 9 = ____

8 x 9 = ____

6 x 9 = ____

A.

B. 5 x 10 = ____

3 x 10 = ____

10 x 10 = ____

7 x 10 = ____

0 x 10 = ____

2 x 10 = ____

6 x 10 = ____

1 x 10 = ____

8 x 10 = ____

9 x 10 = ____

4 x 10 = ____

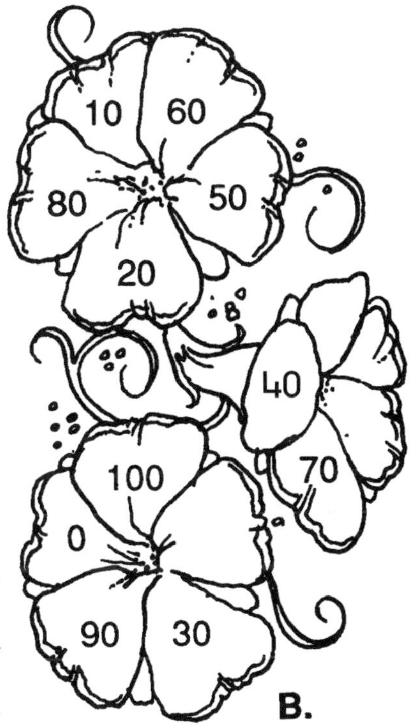

B.

Solve each problem.

C. 9 x 9	**D.** 10 x 0	**E.** 9 x 3	**F.** 10 x 4	**G.** 9 x 8	**H.** 10 x 6
I. 9 x 6	**J.** 9 x 1	**K.** 10 x 5	**L.** 9 x 7	**M.** 10 x 9	**N.** 10 x 10
O. 10 x 3	**P.** 9 x 2	**Q.** 9 x 4	**R.** 10 x 8	 Score ____ / 38	

Brainwork! Look at your answers for problems with 9 as a factor. If you add the digits in each answer, what number will you always get?

Terrific Tens

Skill: Multiplying by multiples of 10

Name ______________________________

Multiply.

A. 6 x 1 = _____

6 x 10 = _____

B. 3 x 4 = _____

3 x 40 = _____

C. 5 x 7 = _____

5 x 70 = _____

D. 8 x 2 = _____

8 x 20 = _____

E. 6 x 6 = _____

6 x 60 = _____

F. 9 x 6 = _____

9 x 60 = _____

G. 4 x 7 = _____

40 x 7 = _____

H. 8 x 5 = _____

8 x 50 = _____

I. 9 x 3 = _____

90 x 3 = _____

J. 7 x 3 = _____

7 x 30 = _____

K. 5 x 5 = _____

50 x 5 = _____

L. 7 x 0 = _____

70 x 0 = _____

M. 4 x 8 = _____

4 x 80 = _____

N. 3 x 6 = _____

30 x 6 = _____

O. 8 x 8 = _____

80 x 8 = _____

Solve each problem.

P. 20 x 9	**Q.** 20 x 3	**R.** 30 x 5	**S.** 40 x 4	**T.** 50 x 2	**U.** 90 x 9
V. 80 x 9	**W.** 70 x 7	**X.** 40 x 0	**Y.** 10 x 8	 Score ___ / 40	

Brainwork! Use these numbers (3, 4, 6, 8, 30, 40, 60, 80) to write four multiplication problems whose answer is 240.

Happy Hundreds

Skill: Multiplying by multiples of 100

Name ________________________________

Multiply.

A. 4 x 1 = ______

4 x 10 = ______

4 x 100 = ______

B. 7 x 3 = ______

7 x 30 = ______

7 x 300 = ______

C. 9 x 9 = ______

9 x 90 = ______

9 x 900 = ______

D. 5 x 6 = ______

50 x 6 = ______

500 x 6 = ______

E. 8 x 7 = ______

8 x 70 = ______

800 x 7 = ______

F. 6 x 2 = ______

60 x 2 = ______

6 x 200 = ______

G. 8 x 8 = ______

80 x 8 = ______

800 x 8 = ______

H. 4 x 5 = ______

4 x 50 = ______

4 x 500 = ______

Solve each problem.

I. 800 x 6	**J.** 900 x 4	**K.** 500 x 5	**L.** 300 x 8	**M.** 700 x 2	**N.** 400 x 6
O. 200 x 2	**P.** 400 x 8	**Q.** 600 x 7	**R.** 900 x 0	**S.** 300 x 6	**T.** 400 x 2
U. 100 x 7	**V.** 200 x 5	**W.** 600 x 9	**X.** 300 x 3		Score ____ / 40

Brainwork! Study the pattern above. Then solve these problems.

7 x 3,000 = ______ 9,000 x 8 = ______ 2 x 60,000 = ______

Fanciful Flight

Skill: Multiplying 2-digit by 1-digit numbers, regrouping

Name ______________________

Score ____ / 25

Solve each problem by multiplying. Cross off the answer on the butterfly.

67 x 5 = **335**	**A.** 19 x 2	**B.** 34 x 8	**C.** 63 x 9	**D.** 15 x 8
E. 49 x 5	**F.** 53 x 6	**G.** 27 x 4	**H.** 37 x 3	**I.** 28 x 7
J. 48 x 9	**K.** 65 x 3	**L.** 17 x 7	**M.** 88 x 2	**N.** 61 x 6
O. 86 x 8	**P.** 24 x 4	**Q.** 55 x 5	**R.** 31 x 9	**S.** 56 x 7

T. 36 x 3	**U.** 42 x 6	**V.** 93 x 4
W. 85 x 2	**X.** 39 x 7	**Y.** 19 x 8

Brainwork! If Dawn saw 13 butterflies and each had 6 spots on its wings, how many butterfly spots did she see?

Up, Up and Away

Skill: Multiplying by 2-digit numbers

Name ______________________

Multiply. Put the letters of the answers on the lines below to find out a secret message.

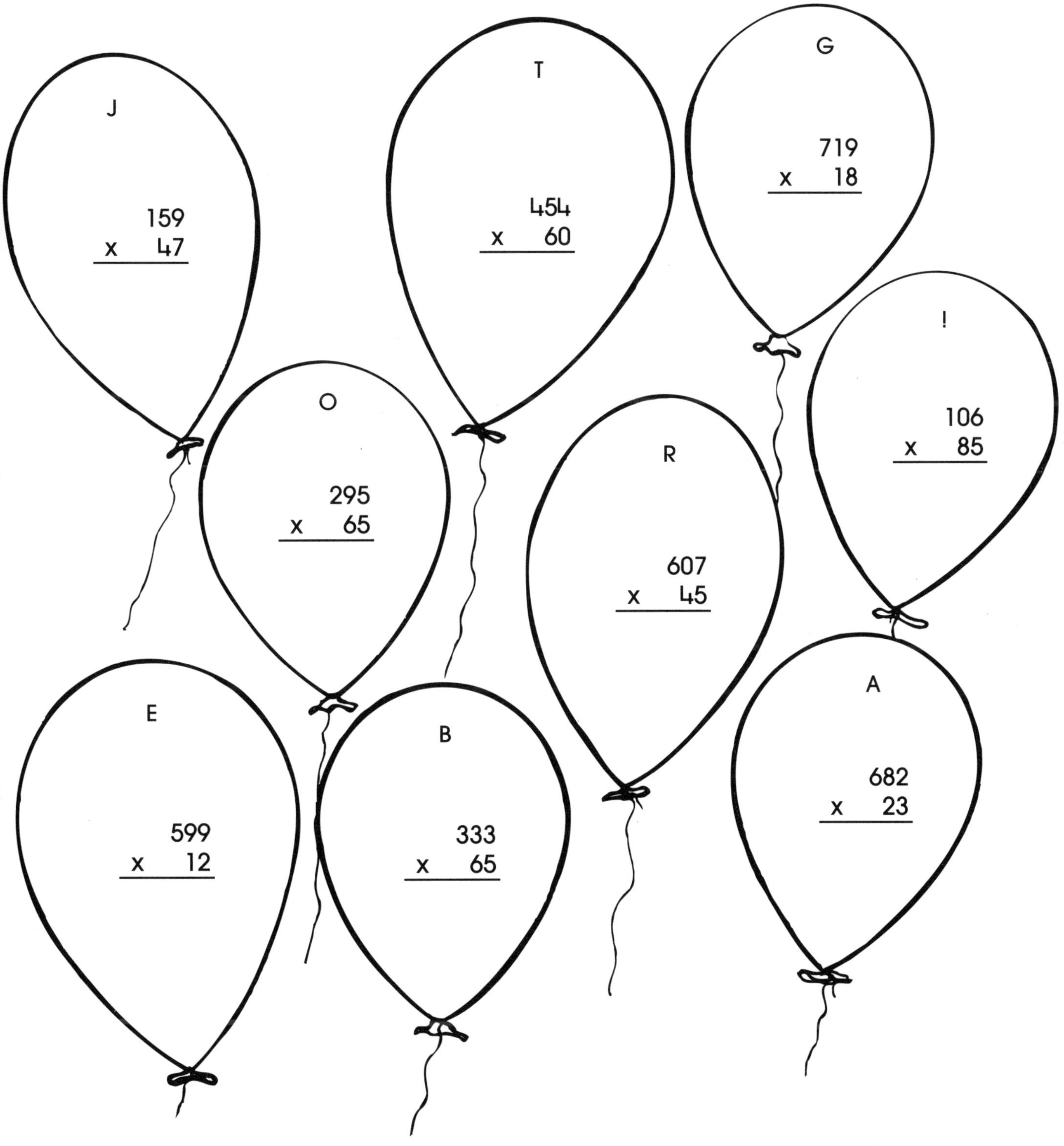

___	___	___	___	___		___	___	___	___
12,942	27,315	7,188	15,686	27,240		7,473	19,175	21,645	9,010

Get in Shape

Skill: Multiplying by 2-digit numbers

Name ______________________

Multiply.

A.

79 x 21	34 x 67	57 x 60	29 x 16

B.

603 x 19	101 x 38	900 x 35	816 x 68

C.

144 x 30	175 x 14	809 x 24	96 x 25

D.

961 x 40	506 x 12	56 x 22	63 x 18

Digit Disease

Skill: Multiplication: 3 Digits x 2 Digits

Name ______________________________

Multiply. Then add the products.

674 × 27	450 × 65	917 × 25	542 × 73	406 × 26
853 × 74	346 × 54	902 × 48	300 × 46	761 × 25
674 × 27	808 × 34	432 × 59	735 × 74	207 × 98
327 × 58	772 × 48	307 × 59	912 × 79	686 × 68

Name ____________________

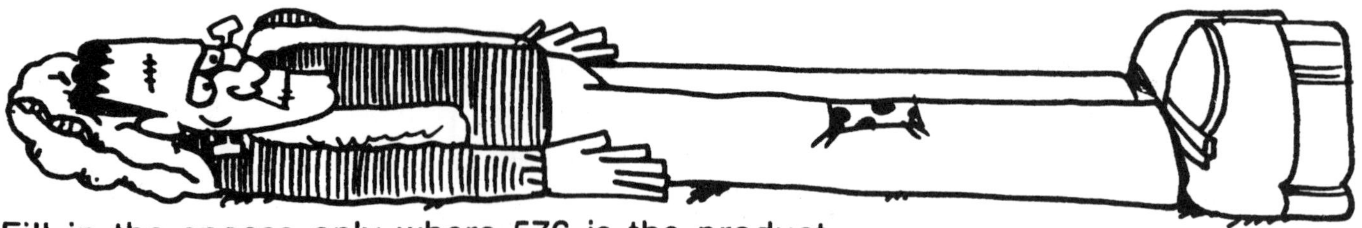

Fill in the spaces only where 576 is the product.

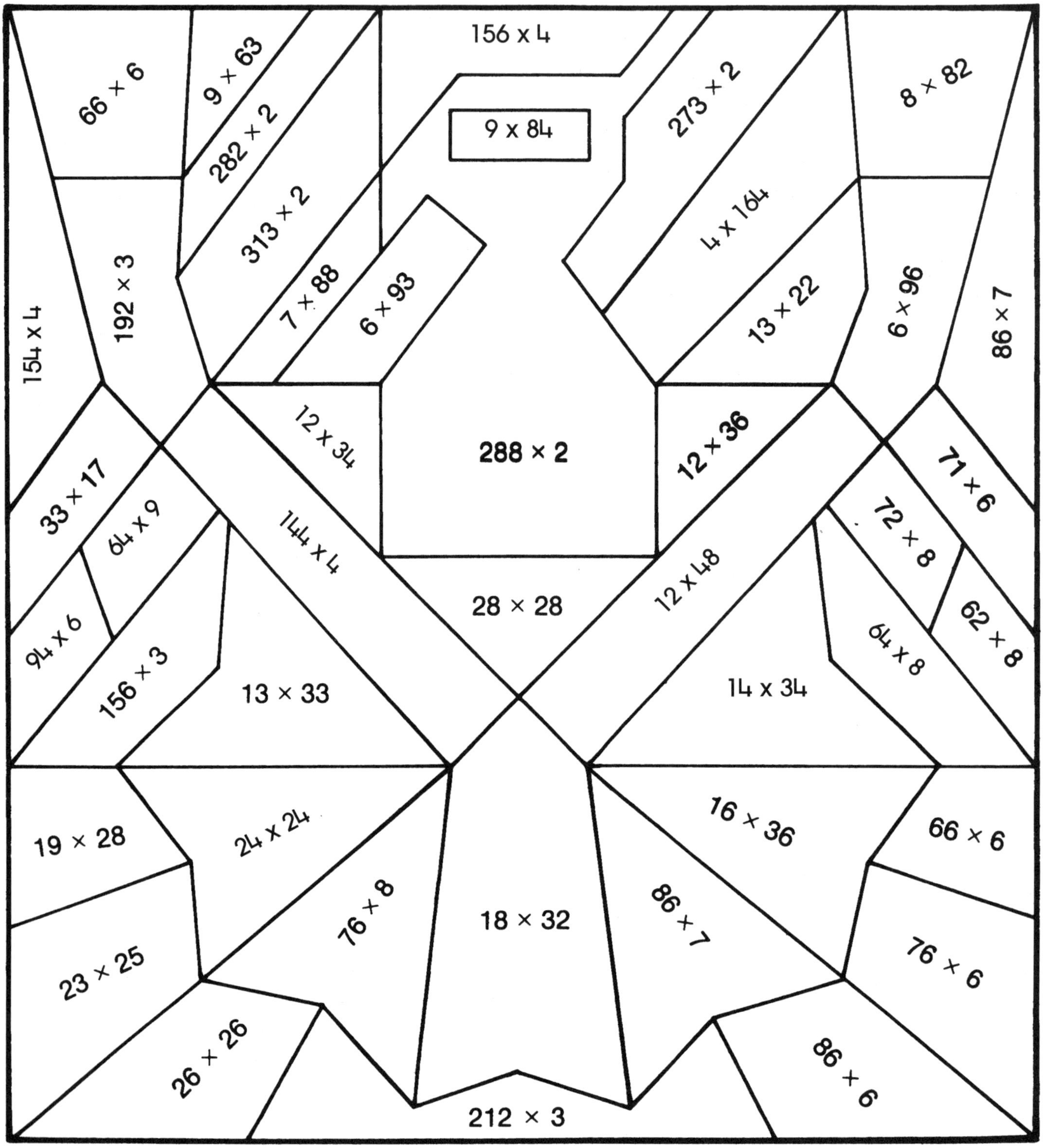

Review

Name ______________________________

When is a bright idea like a clock?

When __ __   __ __ __ __ __ __ __   __ __ __
1 2   3 4 5 6 7 8 9   10 11 12

Directions: Solve each division problem. Find the quotient and matching letter in the code box below to answer the riddle.

1. 4) 72	**2.** 3) 1458	**3.** 7) 161	**4.** 6) 2916
5. 2) 94	**6.** 9) 162	**7.** 5) 385	**8.** 4) 2756
9. 5) 115	**10.** 8) 464	**11.** 6) 150	**12.** 9) 6201

18	23	25	47	58	77	486	689
i	**s**	**n**	**r**	**o**	**k**	**t**	**e**

Get Your Facts Straight

Name ______________________________

Skill: Special products

Complete each equation with a different factor pair. (Hint: Use multiplication facts to help you.)

A. 800

10 x 80

____ x ____

____ x ____

B. 1,000

____ x ____

____ x ____

____ x ____

C. 1,500

____ x ____

____ x ____

____ x ____

D. 1,200

____ x ____

____ x ____

____ x ____

____ x ____

E. 16,000

____ x ____

____ x ____

____ x ____

____ x ____

F. 20,000

____ x ____

____ x ____

____ x ____

____ x ____

G. 4,000

____ x ____

____ x ____

____ x ____

____ x ____

H. 240,000

____ x ____

____ x ____

____ x ____

____ x ____

Shade in the factors that you could NOT use. Then turn your paper so that the right side of the page is at the top. You will see what all of these numbers have in common.

10	40	70	90	70,000	700	30	200	90,000
30	300	700	20	700	60	70	40	9,000
80	500	900	60	9,000	50	400	90	9
7	90	7,000	900	90,000	100	10	20	7,000

Moving Along

Skill: Dividing 1-9

Name ______________________________

Divide each problem. Write the quotient as the divisor for the next problem. Write each final answer in a circle.

1.	5) 25	5) 40	) 56	) 63	) 54	◯
2.	9) 18	) 18	) 81	) 72	) 64	◯
3.	4) 36	) 27	) 21	) 63	) 36	◯
4.	5) 40	) 16	) 16	) 24	) 18	◯
5.	6) 30	) 45	) 45	) 10	) 8	◯
6.	7) 35	) 20	) 32	) 24	) 21	◯
7.	2) 4	) 10	) 15	) 18	) 30	◯
8.	5) 35	) 14	) 16	) 64	) 32	◯

Shade in the answers that are correct.

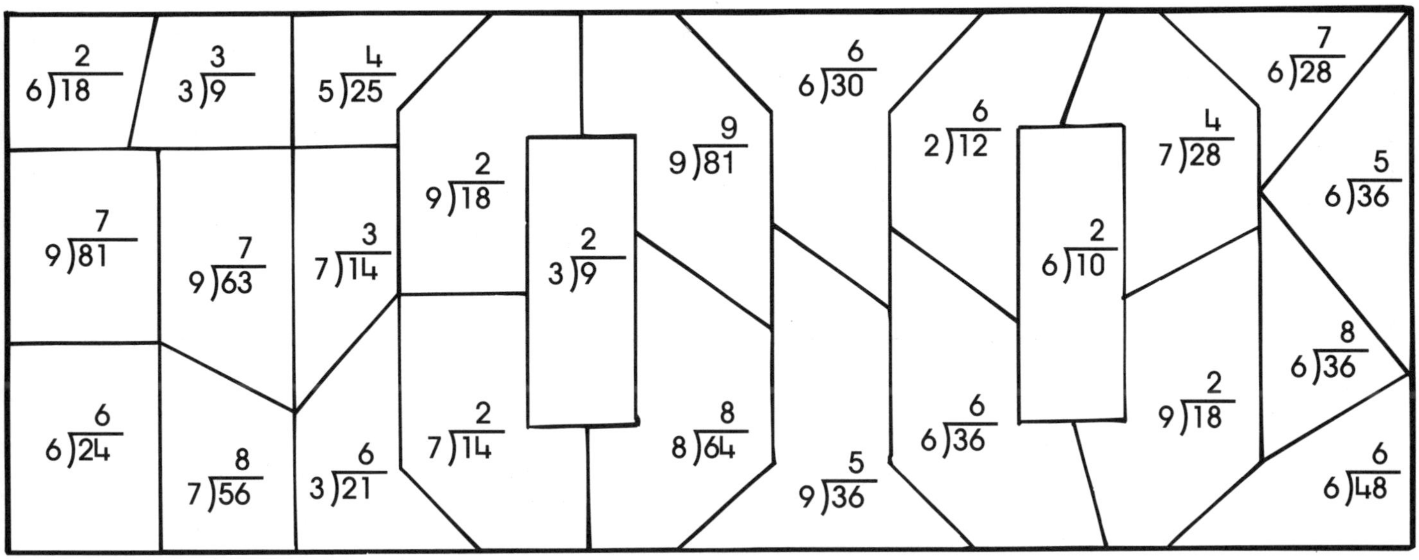

A Riddle

Name ____________________

Skill: Division, divisors of 1, 7

Riddle: Why are elephants so wrinkled?

__ __ __ __   __ __ __   __ __ __ __
4 1 0 5   12 9 8   5 0 5 6

__ __ __ __ __   __ __   __ __ __ __   __ __ __ ?
3 6 10 5 7   3 9   10 6 9 2   9 2 5

A 7 ⟌ 7	D 7 ⟌ 49	E 7 ⟌ 35	H 7 ⟌ 28
I 1 ⟌ 10	N 7 ⟌ 14	O 7 ⟌ 63	R 7 ⟌ 42
T 7 ⟌ 21	U 7 ⟌ 56	V 7 ⟌ 0	Y 1 ⟌ 12

A Riddle

Name ______________________________

Skill: Division, divisors of 1, 6, 7

How do you send a letter to a fish?

__ __ __ __   __ __ __   __ __ S __   __   __ __ __ __.

9 10 6 12   11 3 8   5 2   3   7   4 2 1 8

A 6 ⟌ 42	D 6 ⟌ 54	E 7 ⟌ 56	F 7 ⟌ 35
H 6 ⟌ 18	I 7 ⟌ 14	L 7 ⟌ 28	N 6 ⟌ 6
O 7 ⟌ 42	P 6 ⟌ 72	R 1 ⟌ 10	T 7 ⟌ 77

Cactus Fun!

Name ______________________________

Skill: Division, divisors of 5, 6, 7

DAFFYNITION: A Cactus

___   ___ ___ ___ ___ ___ ___   ___ ___ ___ ___ ___ ___ ___ ___ ___ ___

1   7 5 1 2 0   10 5 2 4 3 8 6 5 9 2

A $5\overline{)5}$	C $6\overline{)24}$	G $7\overline{)49}$	H $6\overline{)36}$
I $6\overline{)30}$	N $5\overline{)10}$	O $7\overline{)63}$	P $5\overline{)50}$
S $7\overline{)56}$	T $6\overline{)0}$	U $5\overline{)15}$	W $5\overline{)55}$

Fruit Fun!

Name ______________________________

Skill: Division, divisors of 1, 7, 8

Daffynition:

__ __ __ __ __ __ : __ __ __ __ __ __ __ __
9 2 4 10 4 5 : 2 0 3 9 9 4 6 8

__ __ __ __ __
1 9 2 7 6

A $8\overline{)16}$	D $8\overline{)64}$	E $8\overline{)48}$	G $7\overline{)7}$
I $8\overline{)32}$	N $7\overline{)35}$	O $7\overline{)21}$	P $7\overline{)49}$
R $8\overline{)72}$	S $1\overline{)10}$	W $8\overline{)0}$	Y $8\overline{)88}$

A Tongue Twister

Name ________________________

Skill: Division, divisors of 8, 9

__ __ __ __ __ __ __   __ __ __ __ __ __
3 8 4 12 10 0 7   6 4 5 3 8 2

__ __ __ __ __ __   __ __ __   __ __ __ __ __ __ __
3 5 3 3 8 2   7 5 9   6 4 5 3 8 2 1

__ __ __ __ __ __ __.
3 5 3 3 8 2 1

B $24 \div 8$ (8 ⟌ 24)	D $54 \div 9$ (9 ⟌ 54)	E $16 \div 8$ (8 ⟌ 16)	G $63 \div 9$ (9 ⟌ 63)
I $10 \div 1$ (1 ⟌ 10)	L $72 \div 9$ (9 ⟌ 72)	M $81 \div 9$ (9 ⟌ 81)	N $0 \div 8$ (8 ⟌ 0)
O $36 \div 9$ (9 ⟌ 36)	S $8 \div 8$ (8 ⟌ 8)	U $45 \div 9$ (9 ⟌ 45)	W $12 \div 1$ (1 ⟌ 12)

Apple Division

Name ______________________________

Skill: Division, basic facts with remainders

How can you divide 19 apples equally among 9 boys?

Write each quotient and remainder.

r : remainder

5) 12 = 2 r 2	3) 10
2) 17	4) 38
4) 33	2) 9
3) 23	5) 41
2) 11	4) 10
4) 25	2) 17
5) 33	3) 20
3) 28	5) 9
	4) 29

6) 14	
9) 75	8) 75
8) 13	6) 50
7) 37	9) 89
9) 30	8) 30
6) 11	7) 19
7) 57	6) 55
8) 58	8) 66
7) 50	7) 48
6) 39	9) 46
9) 55	6) 33

Make applesauce, of course!

A-Mazing Division

Name ______________________________

Skill: 1- and 2-digit quotients with and without remainders

Divide. Check by multiplying.

1. $8 \overline{)480}$ = 60 (check: 60 x 8)
2. $9 \overline{)369}$
3. $5 \overline{)250}$
4. $7 \overline{)560}$
5. $6 \overline{)240}$
6. $4 \overline{)364}$

Divide. Watch out for remainders.

7. $9 \overline{)60}$
8. $8 \overline{)47}$
9. $8 \overline{)75}$
10. $4 \overline{)31}$
11. $3 \overline{)23}$
12. $8 \overline{)47}$

Follow your answers through the maze.

Start ↓

60	41	50	80	30	70	91	13	14
40	4R6	5R1	40	91	6R6	8R2	9R1	3R2
70	18	24	6R1	4R2	5R7	7R4	8R2	9R3
5R5	7R3	6R5	5R2	9R1	9R3	7R3	7R2	5R7

↓ You did it!

Banana Boat

Skill: Dividing 3-digit numbers

Name ______________________________

Divide and write the quotients in the puzzle. Hint: R for remainder will take up its own space.

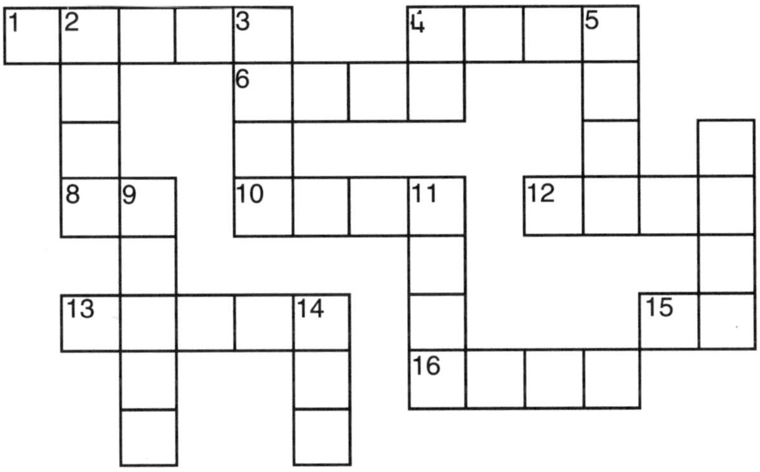

ACROSS

1. $6\overline{)789}$
4. $6\overline{)332}$
6. $4\overline{)291}$
8. $9\overline{)189}$
10. $7\overline{)200}$
12. $8\overline{)651}$
13. $2\overline{)827}$
15. $6\overline{)222}$
16. $5\overline{)396}$

DOWN

2. $6\overline{)188}$
3. $8\overline{)298}$
4. $4\overline{)212}$
5. $9\overline{)244}$
7. $8\overline{)511}$
9. $7\overline{)708}$
11. $9\overline{)394}$
14. $4\overline{)432}$

Zero In

Skill: Zeros in quotients

Name ______________________________

Divide. Watch out for the zeros.

1. 3)914	2. 7)765	3. 8)6472
4. 6)609	5. 5)800	6. 9)975

Write the quotients above in order from smallest to largest.

1. ________ 2. ________ 3. ________ 4. ________ 5. ________ 6. ________

Write the missing digits in each problem.

7.
5□ R 2
5)
2□
□

8.
83□
6)
4□
1□
18
□

9.
5□ R□
4)203
□□
□

10.
9□9
9)8181
□□
□1
□1
0

11.
8□
3)261
□□
□□
21
□

12.
5□1 R□
5)2□09
2□
0□
5
□

13.
□□
8)656
64
16
□□
□

14.
2□□
7)1435
□□
□□
□□
□

Divide It Up

Skill: Dividing by 2-digit numbers

Name ______________________________

Divide. Write the letter of each problem above its answer below.

I. $34\overline{)2584}$	I. $42\overline{)8526}$	O. $63\overline{)6237}$	D. $55\overline{)3575}$
D. $89\overline{)6319}$	Y. $90\overline{)1800}$	T. $31\overline{)6231}$	U. $18\overline{)882}$

___ ___ ___   ___ ___ ___   ___ ___ !

20 99 49   65 203 71   76 201

Find the total test scores below. Then find the averages.

Students	Test Scores					Total	Average
Sue Ann	18	20	17	19	16		
James	15	14	17	16	13		
Tommy	19	19	20	18	19		
Carlos	16	19	18	17	16		
Anna	20	20	19	20	19		

Who has the highest average? ______________

Who needs to study more? ______________

Doggie Trouble

Skill: Dividing by 2-digit numbers with remainders

Name ____________________________________

Help the dog get to his bone by connecting the correctly-done division problems to make a path.

85 R17 23)1972	30 R29 32) 989	14 R27 43) 629	232 R3 30)6963	107 R4 65)6959
104 R8 15)1508	31 R4 22) 687	31 R12 19) 582	78 R6 87)6933	155 R11 52)8071
255 R15 31) 8013	14 R15 42) 6231	20 R18 26) 541	54 R9 18) 819	31 R3 26)809
52 R27 60) 3207	158 R31 39) 6193	36 R11 27) 983	115 R8 71) 8203	58 R3 17)989
		18 R26 81)1484	44 R7 44) 1943	63 R9 28) 1773

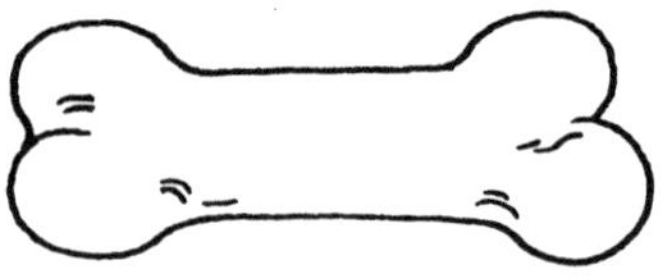

Long Division

Skill: Long division: 2-digit dividend

Name ______________________________

2)72 = 36 6 12 12	8)96	6)84	7)91	3)87
2)74	5)90	7)84	6)96	5)75

Find the quotients and remainders.

5)68	2)71	6)79	7)94	4)75
3)74	6)94	3)47	7)99	6)88

Caterpillar Division

Skill: Long division: 3-digit dividend

Name ______________________________

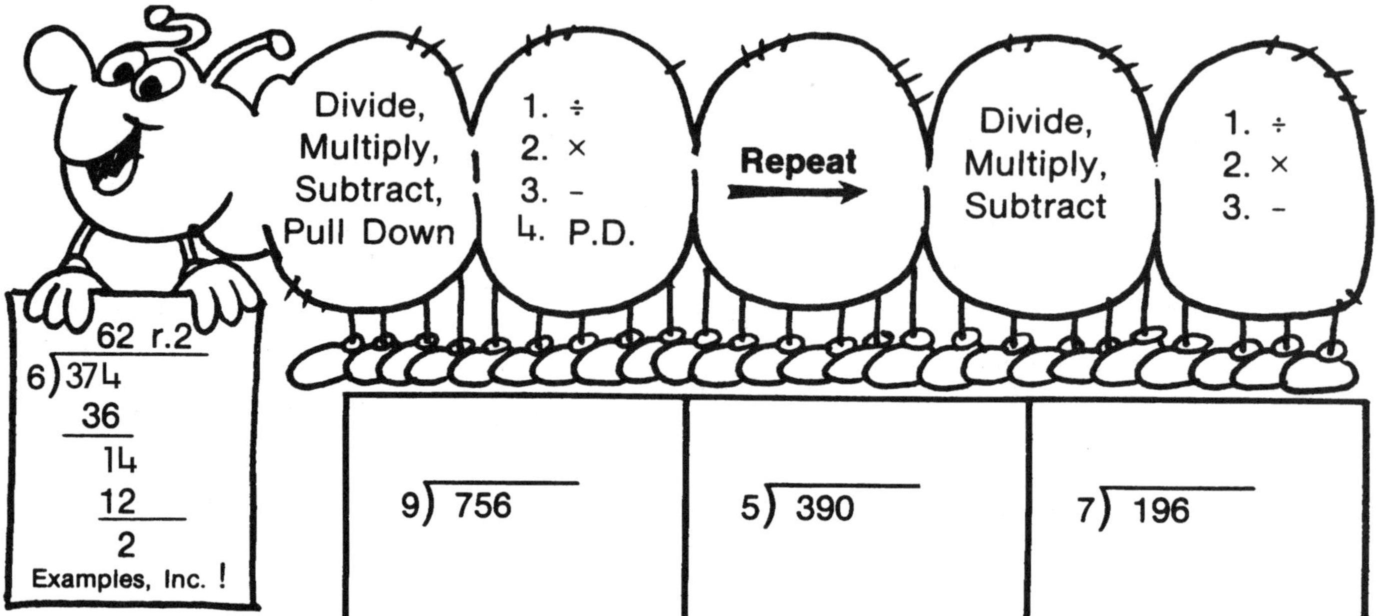

Find the quotients.

	9) 756	5) 390	7) 196
4) 304	3) 201	8) 512	6) 222

Find the quotients and remainders.

4) 187	8) 339	7) 268	3) 176
4) 400	6) 215	9) 319	4) 107

Snake Parts

Skill: Writing fractions

Name ____________________

Write fractions for:

one-half ______ one-third ______ one-fifth ______

one-fourth ______ one-sixth ______ one-tenth ______

one-eighth ______ one-twelfth ______ one-seventh ______

Write fractions for:

one of four parts ______ one of nine parts ______

one of three parts ______ one of six parts ______

one of two parts ______ one of five parts ______

Colour each part as directed.

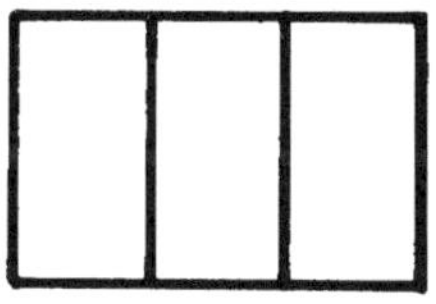

Colour $\frac{1}{3}$ blue.

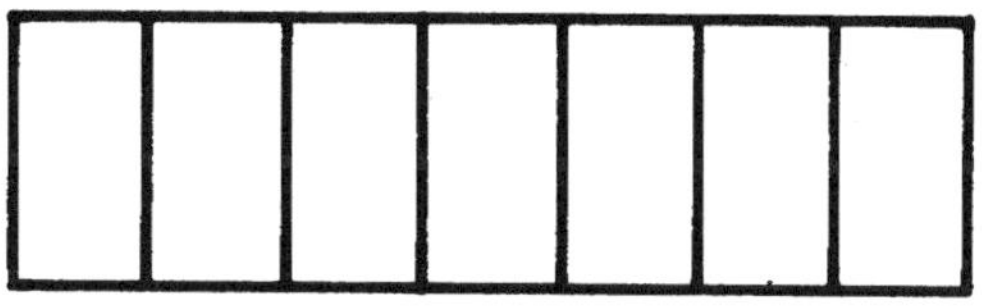

Colour $\frac{1}{7}$ yellow.

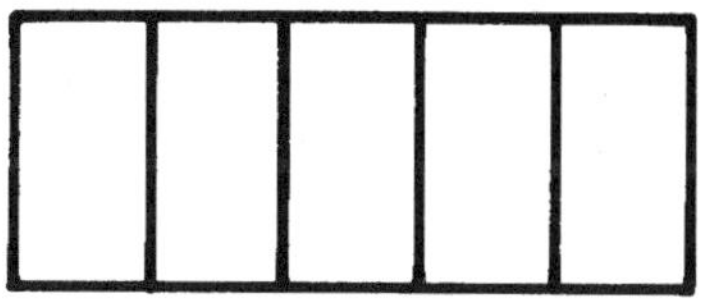

Colour $\frac{1}{5}$ red.

Colour $\frac{1}{4}$ green.

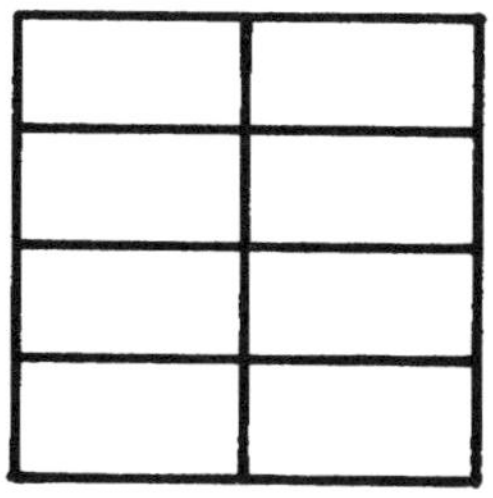

Colour $\frac{1}{8}$ orange.

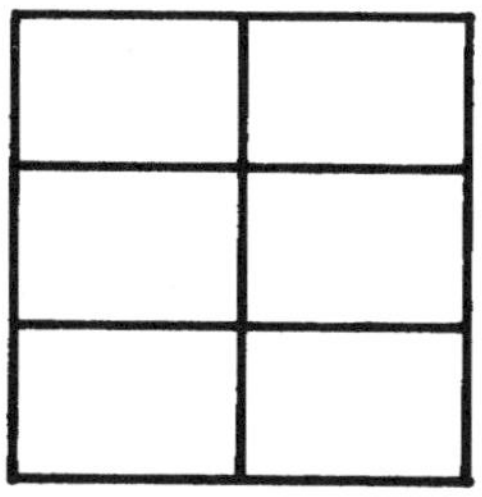

Colour $\frac{1}{6}$ brown.

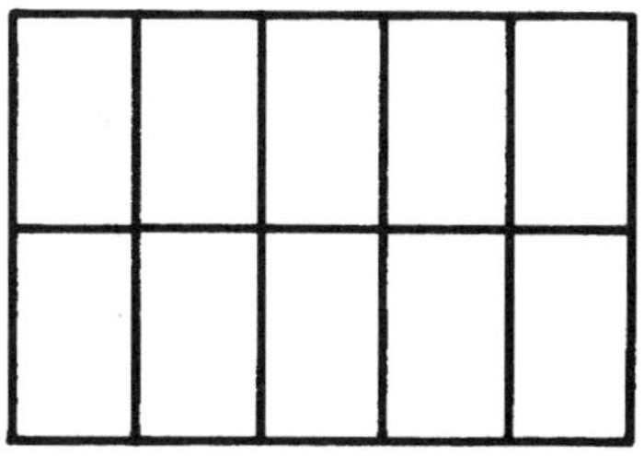

Colour $\frac{1}{10}$ black.

Pizza Fractions

Skill: Writing fractions

Name ______________________________

$\frac{3}{5}$ ← 3 parts are shaded.

There are 5 equal parts. → 5

Write the fraction for the following shaded parts.

Use These Fractions

$\frac{1}{2}$ $\frac{1}{3}$ $\frac{2}{3}$ $\frac{2}{8}$ $\frac{3}{8}$ $\frac{4}{8}$

$\frac{1}{4}$ $\frac{2}{4}$ $\frac{3}{4}$ $\frac{3}{5}$ $\frac{4}{5}$ $\frac{1}{6}$ $\frac{4}{6}$ $\frac{5}{6}$ $\frac{5}{7}$ $\frac{7}{8}$ $\frac{5}{9}$ $\frac{5}{10}$

Fraction Pie

Name ____________________________

Skill: Writing and shading fractions

Here are two of three equal parts of this circle.

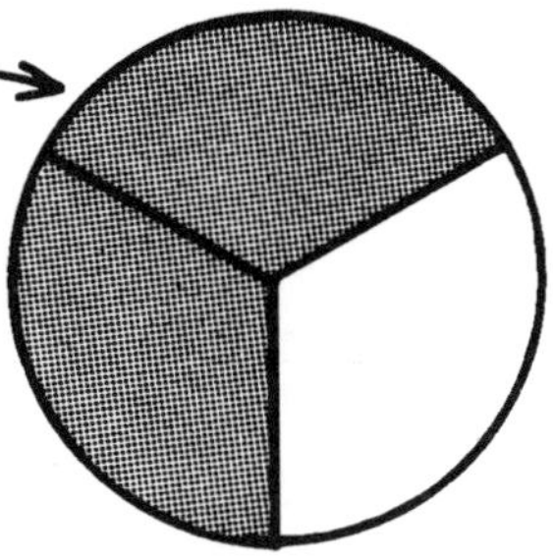

The fraction for "two of three parts" is $\frac{2}{3}$.

Fill in the missing numbers and shade the parts.

"five of six" = $\frac{\quad}{6}$

"one of two"= $\frac{\quad}{2}$

"four of five" = $\frac{4}{\quad}$

"three of four"= $\frac{\quad}{4}$

"three of eight" = $\frac{\quad}{8}$

"two of five"= $\frac{\quad}{5}$

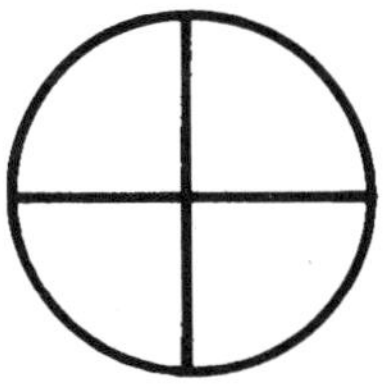

"three of four" = $\frac{3}{\quad}$

"five of eight"= $\frac{5}{\quad}$

"seven of twelve" = $\frac{7}{\quad}$

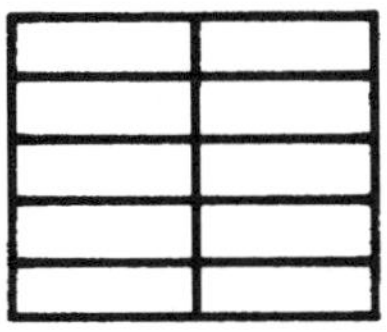

"nine of ten"= $\frac{9}{\quad}$

Snowflake Fun!

Name ______________________________

Skill: Reducing fractions

Reduce the fractions below and write them in word form.

ACROSS

1. $\frac{4}{36}$ = one _____
4. $\frac{4}{28}$ = _____ seventh
5. $\frac{30}{33}$ = _____ elevenths
6. $\frac{9}{12}$ = three _____
8. $\frac{15}{18}$ = five _____
11. $\frac{7}{56}$ = one _____
12. $\frac{16}{36}$ = _____ ninths
13. $\frac{9}{72}$ = _____ eighth
14. $\frac{25}{45}$ = five _____
17. $\frac{24}{33}$ = _____ elevenths

DOWN

1. $\frac{3}{27}$ = one _____
2. $\frac{9}{18}$ = one _____
3. $\frac{20}{35}$ = _____ sevenths
7. $\frac{2}{4}$ = one _____
9. $\frac{9}{21}$ = _____ sevenths
10. $\frac{12}{42}$ = two _____
15. $\frac{8}{24}$ = one _____
16. $\frac{12}{26}$ = _____ thirteenths

Equal Time

Name ______________________________

Skill: Equivalent fractions

To find equivalent fractions, the numerator and denominator are multiplied by the same number.

$$\frac{1\ (\times 3)}{3\ (\times 3)} = \frac{3}{9} \qquad \frac{1\ (\times 6)}{2\ (\times 6)} = \frac{6}{12} \qquad \frac{1\ (\times 2)}{4\ (\times 2)} = \frac{2}{8}$$

Change each fraction to higher terms.

1. $\frac{1\ (\times \square)}{5\ (\times \square)} = \frac{\square}{10}$
2. $\frac{2\ (\times \square)}{5\ (\times \square)} = \frac{\square}{10}$
3. $\frac{1\ (\times \square)}{6\ (\times \square)} = \frac{\square}{12}$
4. $\frac{2\ (\times \square)}{7\ (\times \square)} = \frac{\square}{21}$
5. $\frac{1\ (\times \square)}{2\ (\times \square)} = \frac{\square}{12}$
6. $\frac{2\ (\times \square)}{3\ (\times \square)} = \frac{\square}{12}$

Multiply in your head. If the equivalents are correct, shade in the areas.

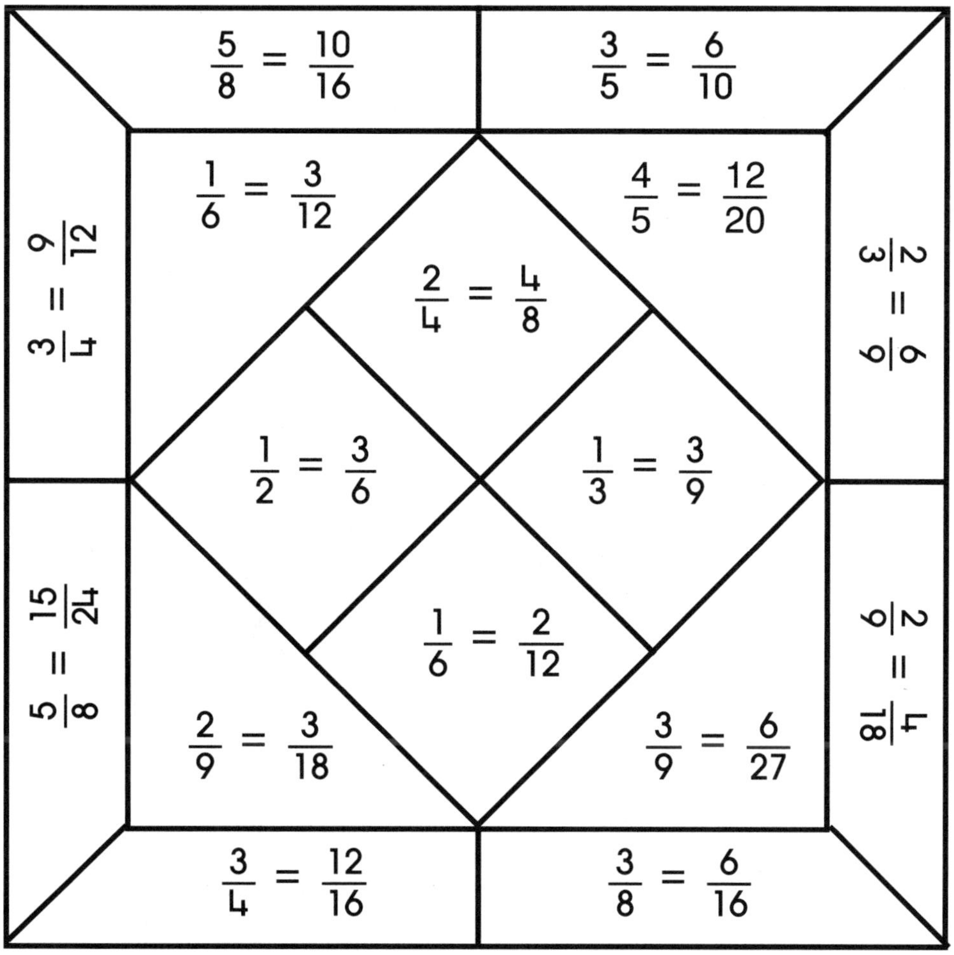

Bubble Fun

Skill: Improper fractions and mixed numbers

Name ______________________________

Change each improper fraction to a mixed number. Or, change each mixed number to an improper fraction.

1. $\frac{17}{8}$
2. $1\frac{1}{4}$
3. $\frac{13}{4}$
4. $2\frac{1}{5}$
5. $\frac{47}{9}$
6. $4\frac{2}{5}$
7. $\frac{15}{4}$
8. $3\frac{5}{9}$
9. $4\frac{5}{9}$
10. $\frac{25}{5}$
11. $5\frac{1}{8}$
12. $\frac{12}{3}$
13. $8\frac{7}{9}$
14. $\frac{67}{9}$
15. $\frac{37}{6}$
16. $7\frac{3}{5}$
17. $\frac{83}{5}$
18. $\frac{39}{7}$

Let's Compare

Skill: Comparing fractions

Name ______________________________

Use >, <, or = to compare the fractions below.

A. $\frac{11}{12}$ ○ $\frac{8}{9}$ $\frac{3}{4}$ ○ $\frac{6}{8}$ $\frac{5}{6}$ ○ $\frac{2}{3}$

B. $\frac{1}{5}$ ○ $\frac{2}{3}$ $\frac{9}{10}$ ○ $\frac{3}{4}$ $\frac{2}{5}$ ○ $\frac{10}{11}$

C. $\frac{2}{5}$ ○ $\frac{8}{20}$ $\frac{1}{4}$ ○ $\frac{3}{8}$ $\frac{7}{9}$ ○ $\frac{3}{4}$

D. $\frac{6}{7}$ ○ $\frac{2}{5}$ $\frac{4}{7}$ ○ $\frac{8}{14}$ $\frac{12}{13}$ ○ $\frac{4}{5}$

Cloud Crazy

Skill: Adding and subtracting fractions with like denominators

Name ______________________________

Add or subtract.

A.

$\frac{3}{5} + \frac{1}{5} =$ ____

$\frac{1}{8} + \frac{4}{8} =$ ____

$\frac{1}{4} + \frac{2}{4} =$ ____

$\frac{5}{8} - \frac{3}{8} =$ ____

B.

$\frac{7}{8} - \frac{3}{8} =$ ____

$\frac{2}{9} + \frac{5}{9} =$ ____

$\frac{3}{4} - \frac{1}{4} =$ ____

$\frac{1}{12} + \frac{3}{12} =$ ____

C.

$\frac{7}{12} - \frac{1}{12} =$ ____

$\frac{3}{8} + \frac{5}{8} =$ ____

$\frac{5}{9} + \frac{1}{9} =$ ____

$\frac{2}{3} - \frac{1}{3} =$ ____

X Marks the Spot

Name ______________________

Skill: Solving proportions

Solve for **x**. Shade in the answers in the box below. Your answers will form a design.

A. $\frac{5}{6} = \frac{\mathbf{x}}{24}$ x = ______ $\frac{1}{4} = \frac{\mathbf{x}}{20}$ x = ______ $\frac{9}{10} = \frac{\mathbf{x}}{50}$ x = ______

B. $\frac{2}{3} = \frac{\mathbf{x}}{18}$ x = ______ $\frac{3}{4} = \frac{\mathbf{x}}{20}$ x = ______ $\frac{4}{7} = \frac{\mathbf{x}}{28}$ x = ______

C. $\frac{3}{8} = \frac{\mathbf{x}}{48}$ x = ______ $\frac{5}{2} = \frac{\mathbf{x}}{10}$ x = ______ $\frac{1}{3} = \frac{\mathbf{x}}{30}$ x = ______

D. $\frac{7}{3} = \frac{\mathbf{x}}{18}$ x = ______ $\frac{7}{9} = \frac{\mathbf{x}}{72}$ x = ______ $\frac{8}{9} = \frac{\mathbf{x}}{36}$ x = ______

E. $\frac{2}{7} = \frac{\mathbf{x}}{49}$ x = ______ $\frac{5}{8} = \frac{\mathbf{x}}{64}$ x = ______ $\frac{9}{10} = \frac{\mathbf{x}}{70}$ x = ______

19	20		63	31
16	13	40	29	12
15	42	23	45	10
14	37	25	11	5
43	18	56	32	17

What is it? ____________

Match Ups

Name ______________________________

Skill: Relating decimals and fractions

Decimals can be used to show tenths. ($0.6 = \frac{6}{10}$) Write the decimals for the shaded parts.

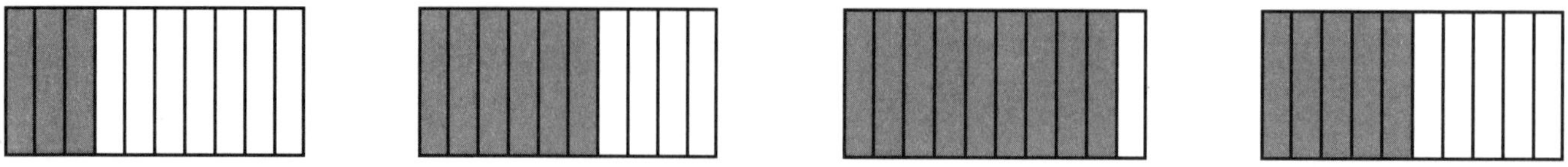

1. ____________ 2. ____________ 3. ____________ 4. ____________

5. Match the decimals with the fractions and word names.

$\frac{8}{10}$	0.4	seven tenths
$\frac{1}{10}$	0.8	four tenths
$\frac{7}{10}$	0.1	eight tenths
$\frac{4}{10}$	0.7	one tenth

Whole numbers are shown before the decimal. Example: two and nine tenths = 2.9
Write the whole numbers and decimals for the shaded figures.

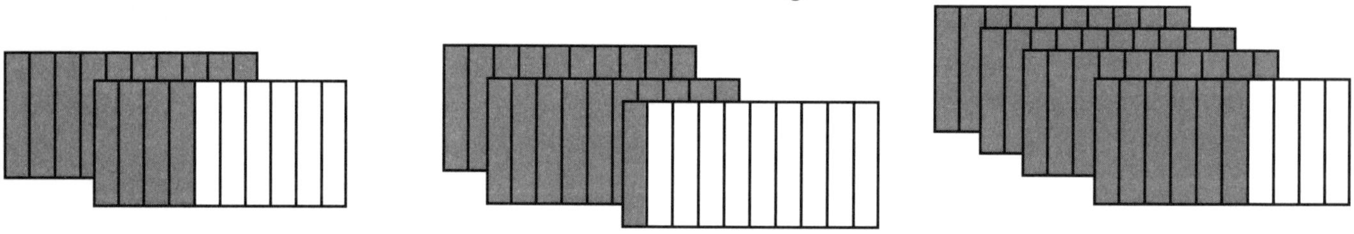

6. ____________ 7. ____________ 8. ____________

Hundredths can be shown using decimals, too. twelve hundredths = 0.12

9. Match the decimals for the shaded parts.

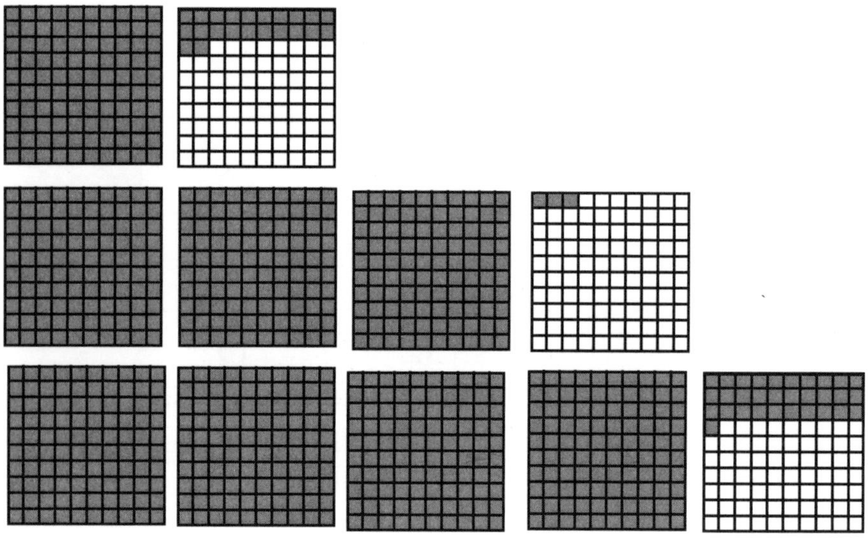

4.31

1.22

3.03

Decimal Dilemma

Skill: Writing and comparing decimals

Name ______________________________

Write the decimals two other ways.

2.06	$2\frac{6}{100}$	two and six hundredths
6.9		
4.73		
0.84		
7.4		

Circle the largest decimal in each section and draw a box around the smallest decimal. If the decimal circled is in the middle of the group, colour the section red. If it is on the right, colour it blue. If it is on the left, leave it white.

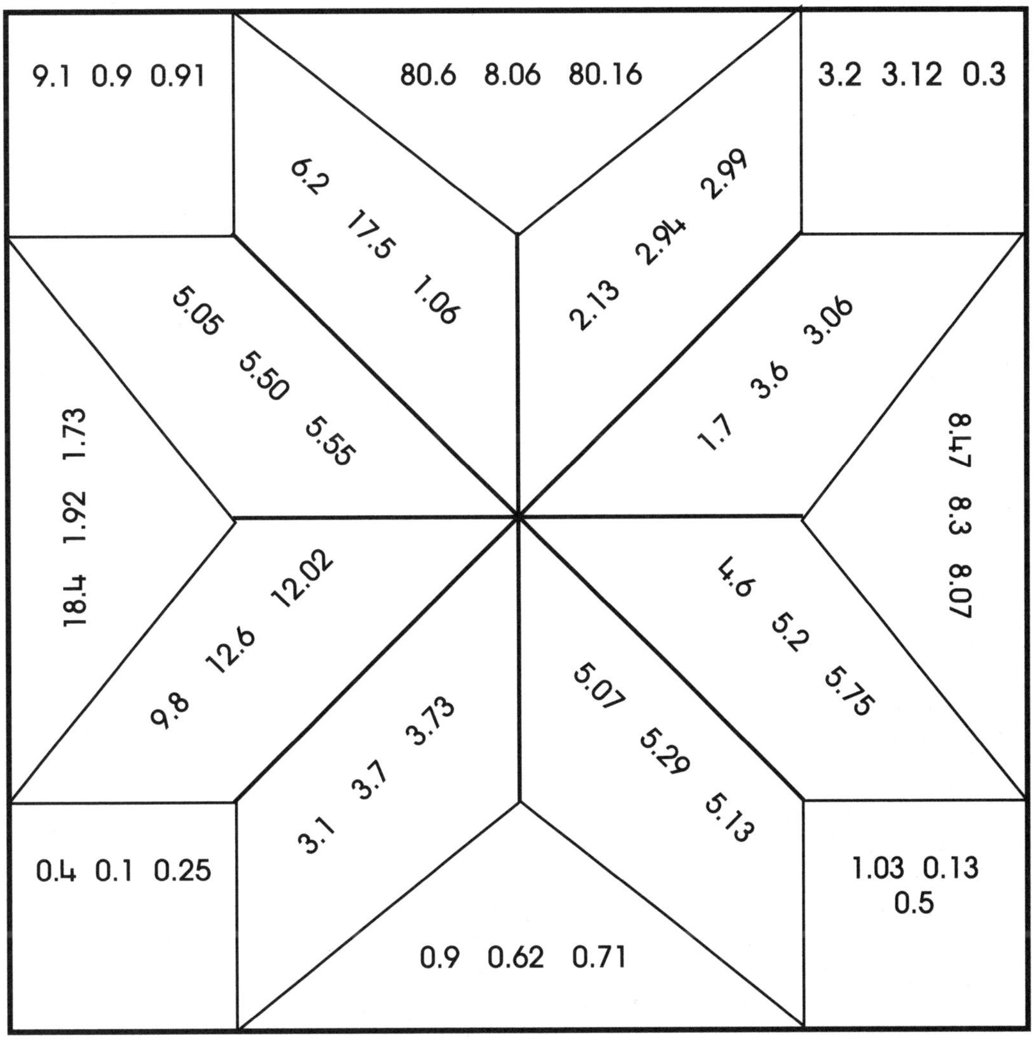

What's Missing?

Name ______________________________

Skill: Adding and subtracting decimals; comparing decimals

Add or subtract.

A.

0.9	5.7	6.04	5.55	10.10	11.7
+ 4.6	− 2.9	+ 3.12	− 4.60	− 4.65	+ 10.1

B.

9.1	51.6	70.99	18.4	9.99	6.71
7.5	27.9	61.73	20.7	2.73	12.58
+ 6.2	+ 18.8	+ 47.12	+ 32.5	+ 1.84	+ 9.01

C. 11.07 + 9.91 =   27.9 − 12.6 =   13.21 − 7.54 =

D. Write the missing digits.

4 . □ 6	□ . 4 6	8 . □ □	9 2 . 7	□ □ . 9
+ 5 . 7 □	− 3 . □ 5	+ 5 . 6 6	− 6 □ . 9	− 3 8 . □
1 □ . 1 0	3 . 5 □	1 □ . 1 0	□ 0 . □	4 1 . 6

E. 5.66 + □.□□ = 9.99   12.6 + □□.□ = 22.9

□.□ − 3.17 = 3.63

F. Shade in the boxes where the decimals are in numerical order.

4.9, 6.2	1.7, 1.6	12.06, 13.2
12.4, 9.6	8.0, 8.01	2.7, 2.67
5.01, 5.35	2.66, 2.65	72.9, 79.2
2.13, 2.03	1.6, 1.7	5.00, 4.9
2.04, 2.14	4.01, 4.00	18.6, 18.65
3.1, 3.01	9.9, 10.01	2.75, 2.70

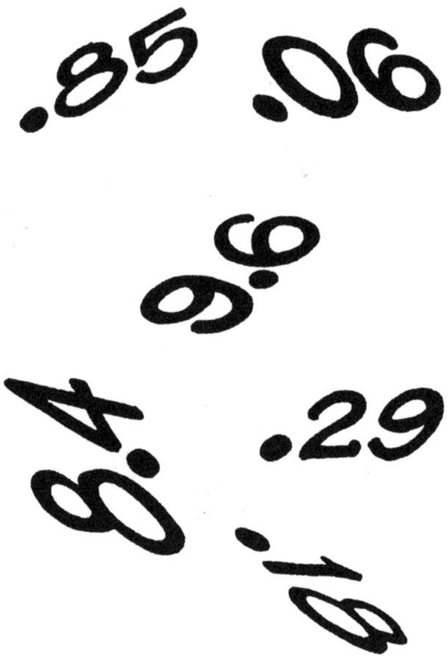

Sweet Treats

Skill: Adding and subtracting decimals

Name ______________________________

Add or subtract.

1.
$$\begin{array}{r} 76.9 \\ +\ 22.36 \\ \hline \end{array}$$

2. 15.98 + 17.9 =

3.
$$\begin{array}{r} 485.6 \\ -\ 13.98 \\ \hline \end{array}$$

4.
$$\begin{array}{r} 103.02 \\ -\ 46.6 \\ \hline \end{array}$$

5.
$$\begin{array}{r} 261.83 \\ -\ 92.7 \\ \hline \end{array}$$

6.
$$\begin{array}{r} 92.6 \\ -\ 8.25 \\ \hline \end{array}$$

7.
$$\begin{array}{r} 29.19 \\ -\ 48.3 \\ \hline \end{array}$$

8. 29.1 − 8.15 =

9.
$$\begin{array}{r} 185.6 \\ +\ 545.83 \\ \hline \end{array}$$

10.
$$\begin{array}{r} 103.7 \\ -\ 17.3 \\ \hline \end{array}$$

11.
$$\begin{array}{r} 603.1 \\ +\ 79.33 \\ \hline \end{array}$$

12. 10.92 + 498.3 =

An Unusual Timepiece

Name ______________________________

Skill: Fractions and percentages

Complete each equation with a ratio or a percentage. Use your answers to find a definition for "a unique timepiece."

A. $\frac{11}{100}$ = ______	A. $\frac{8}{100}$ = ______	A. $\frac{17}{100}$ = ______	A. $\frac{25}{100}$ = ______
A. $\frac{31}{100}$ = ______	E. $\frac{43}{100}$ = ______	E. $\frac{77}{100}$ = ______	I. $\frac{49}{100}$ = ______
I. $\frac{4}{100}$ = ______	O. $\frac{19}{100}$ = ______	O. $\frac{23}{100}$ = ______	W. $\frac{46}{100}$ = ______
G. $\frac{25}{100}$ = ______	T. $\frac{33}{100}$ = ______	D. $\frac{79}{100}$ = ______	T. 14% = ______
L. 67% = ______	M. 58% = ______	C. 53% = ______	C. 28% = ______
H. 12% = ______	H. 71% = ______	N. 17% = ______	T. 39% = ______
S. 84% = ______	T. 47% = ______		
D. 91% = ______	G. 5% = ______		
T. 75% = ______			
L. 2% = ______			

___ 11%   ___ 46% ___ 8% ___ $\frac{75}{100}$ ___ $\frac{28}{100}$ ___ $\frac{71}{100}$ ___ 79% ___ 19% ___ $\frac{5}{100}$

___ 49% ___ $\frac{84}{100}$ ___ 17%   ___ $\frac{91}{100}$ ___ 23% ___ 25%   ___ $\frac{47}{100}$ ___ $\frac{12}{100}$ ___ 25% ___ $\frac{39}{100}$

___ $\frac{53}{100}$ ___ 31% ___ $\frac{17}{100}$ ___ 33% ___ 43% ___ $\frac{2}{100}$ ___ $\frac{67}{100}$ ___ $\frac{14}{100}$ ___ 4% ___ $\frac{58}{100}$ ___ 77% .

Perimeter Problems

Skill: Perimeter

Name ______________________________

What is the highest waterfall in the world?

To find out, find the perimeter of each figure below at the bottom of the page. Write the letter that represents each problem above its answer.

Remember: Perimeter is equal to the sum of the sides of a figure.

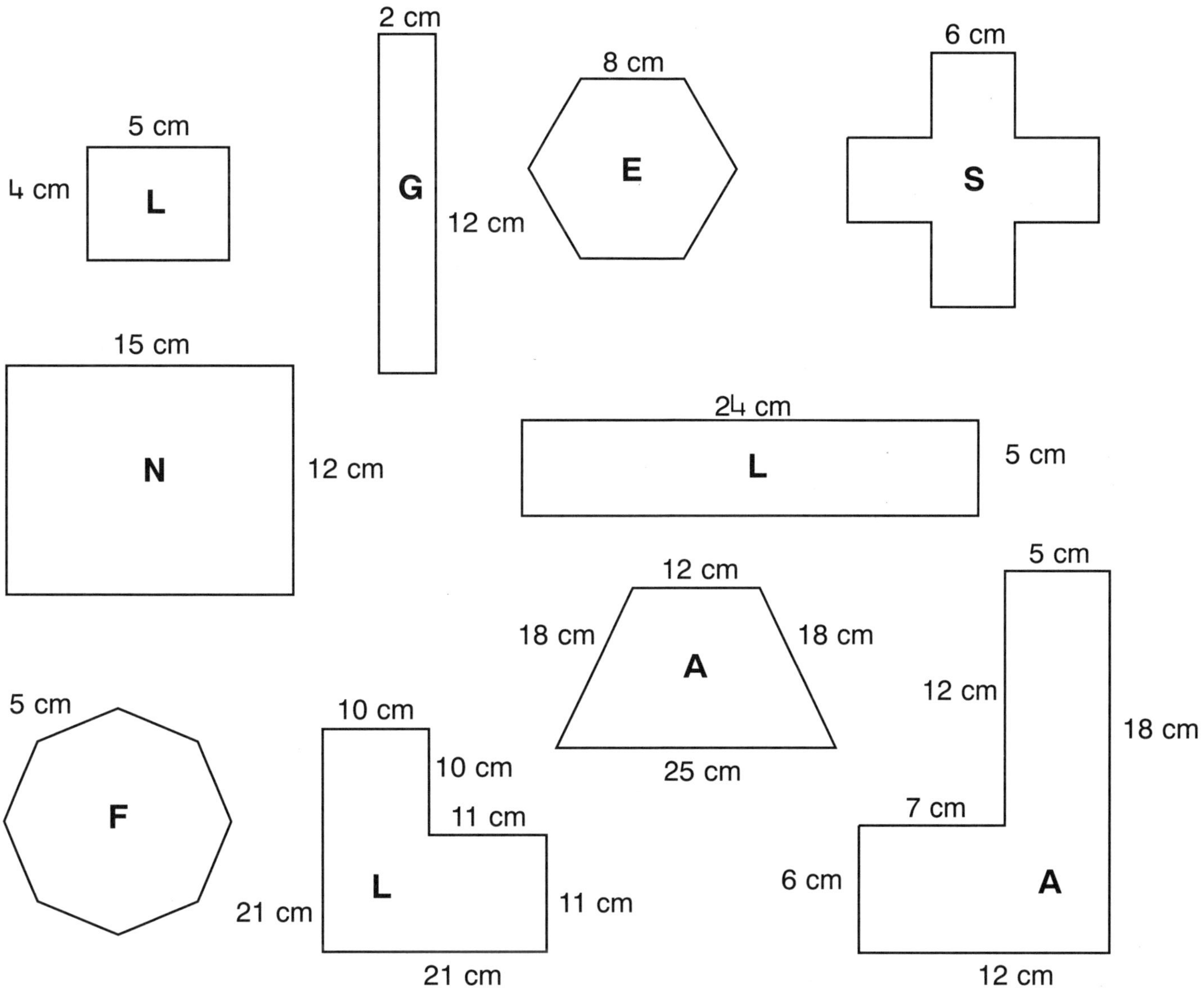

___ 73 cm   ___ 54 cm   ___ 28 cm   ___ 48 cm   ___ 84 cm

___ 40 cm   ___ 60 cm   ___ 18 cm   ___ 58 cm   ___ 72 cm

Amazing Muscles

Skill: Area

Name ______________________________

It takes 17 muscles to smile. How many muscles does it take to frown?

To find out, find the areas at the bottom of the page.
Write the letter that represents each problem above its answer.

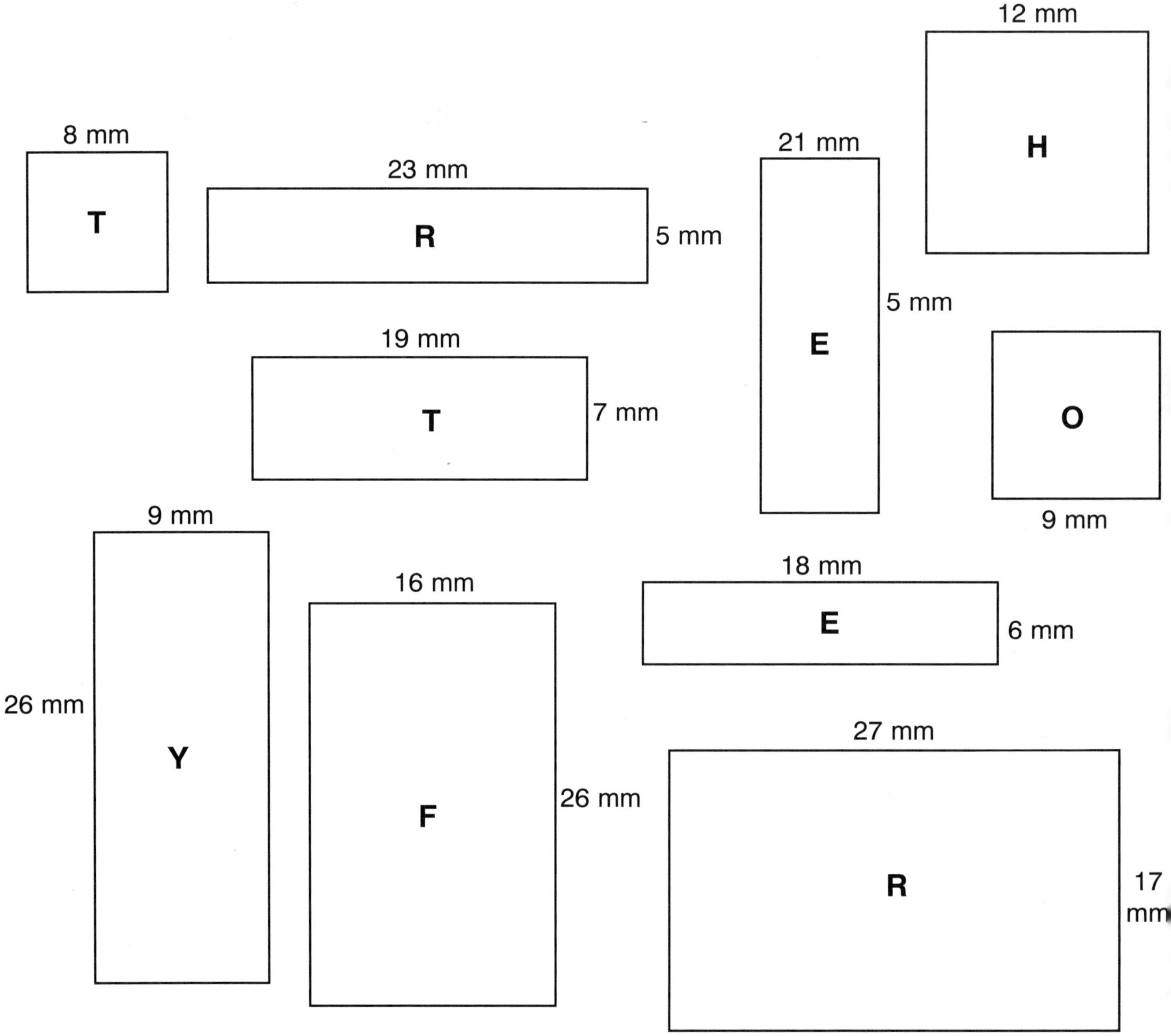

____ ____ ____ ____ ____ – ____ ____ ____ ____ ____

416 mm^2 81 mm^2 459 mm^2 64 mm^2 234 mm^2 – 133 mm^2 144 mm^2 115 mm^2 108 mm^2 105 mm^2

Very Important Volume

Name ______________________________

Skill: Volume

Volume is the number of cubic units that will fit inside a space figure. Build each figure below using linking cubes. Tell the number of cubes used.

1.

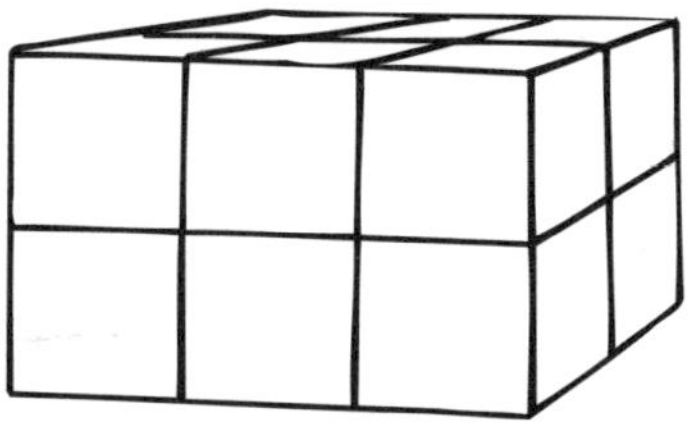

_____ cubic units

2.

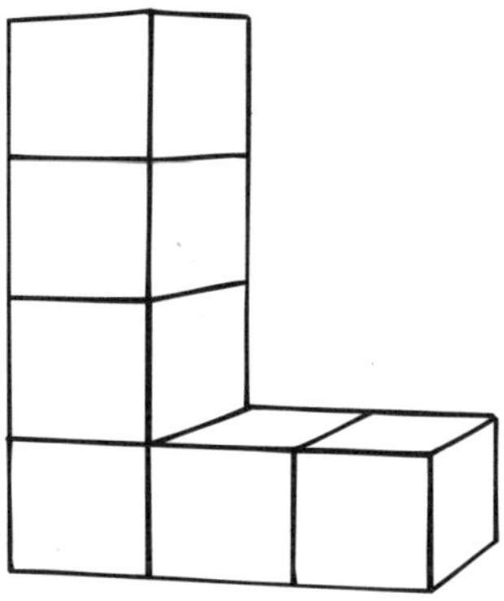

_____ cubic units

3.

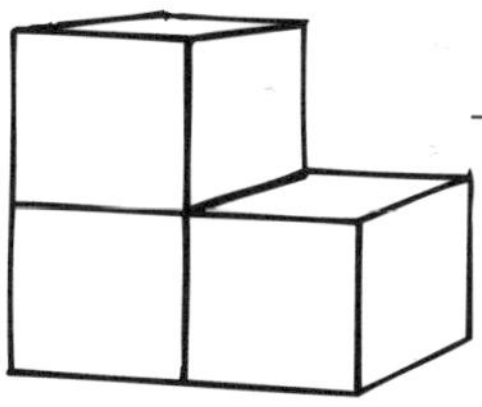

_____ cubic units

Volume can be found by multiplying the length times the width times the height.

V = l x w x h

Find the volume of each figure below.

4.

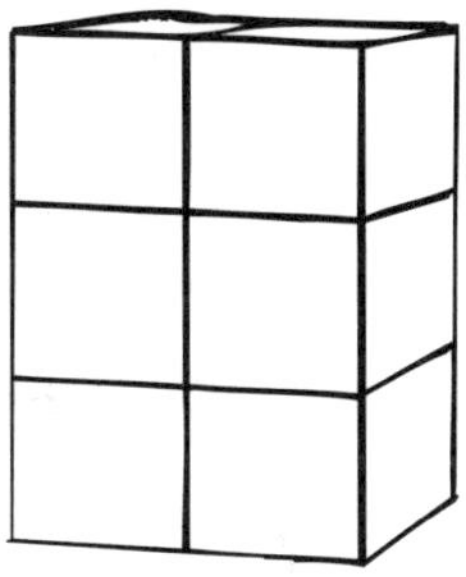

_____ x _____ x _____ = _____ cu. units

5.

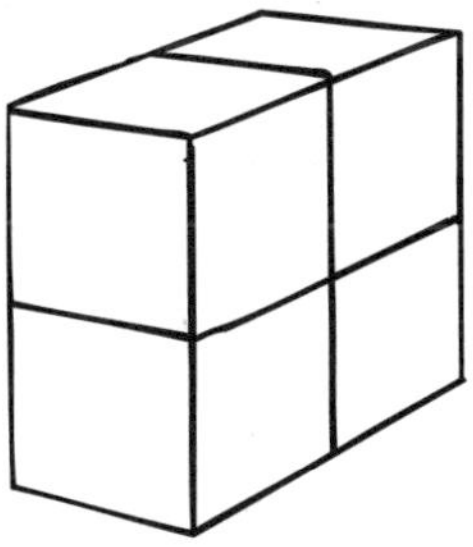

_____ x _____ x _____ = _____ cu. units

6.

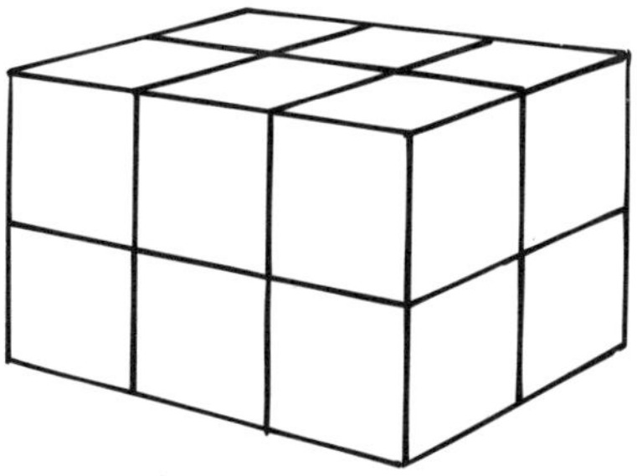

_____ x _____ x _____ = _____ cu. units

7.

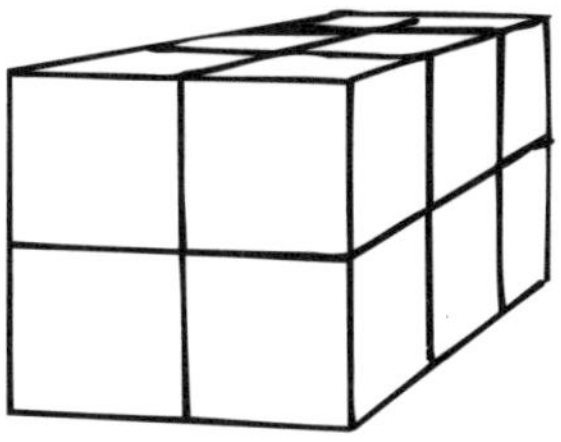

_____ x _____ x _____ = _____ cu. units

8.

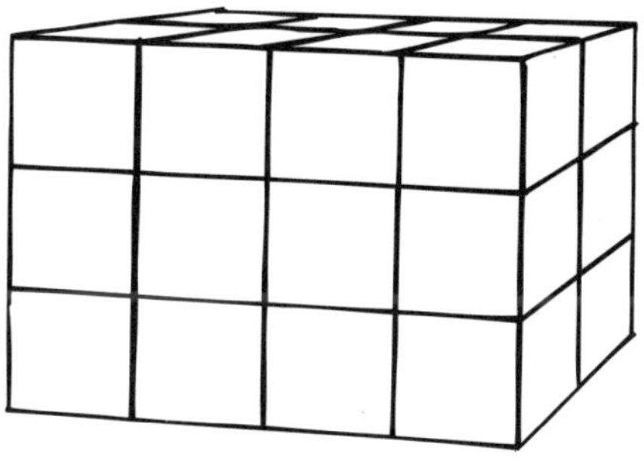

_____ x _____ x _____ = _____ cu. units

9.

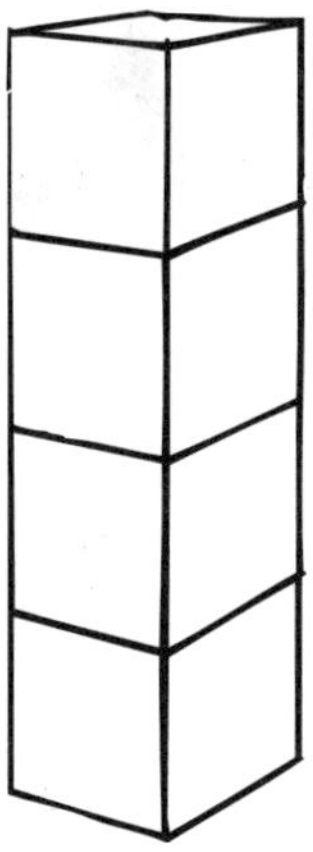

_____ x _____ x

_____ = _____

cu. units

How Hot Is It?

Skill: Temperature - Celsius, Fahrenheit

Name ______________________________

Temperature is measured in degrees Celsius or Fahrenheit.

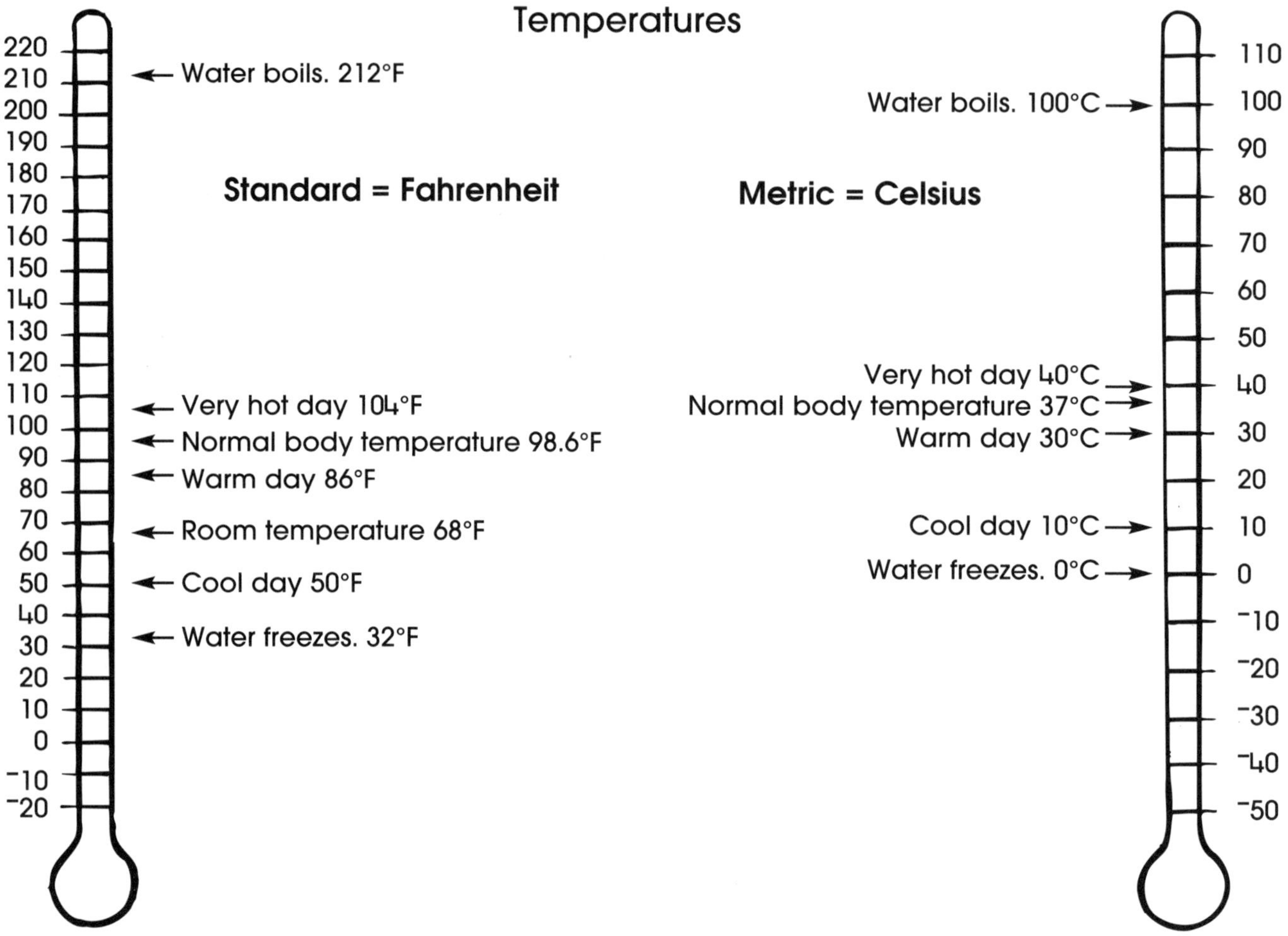

Use the thermometers to show the temperatures below in Celsius and Fahrenheit.

	degrees Fahrenheit	degrees Celsius
Water boils.		
Normal body temperature		
A very hot day		
A warm day		
A cool day		
Water freezes.		

Quadrilateral Riddles

Name ____________________

Skill: Quadrilaterals

Solve each riddle. Then draw it on the geoboard dot paper grids. Use the Word Bank to help you.

Word Bank

kite   parallelogram   rectangle   rhombus   square   trapezium

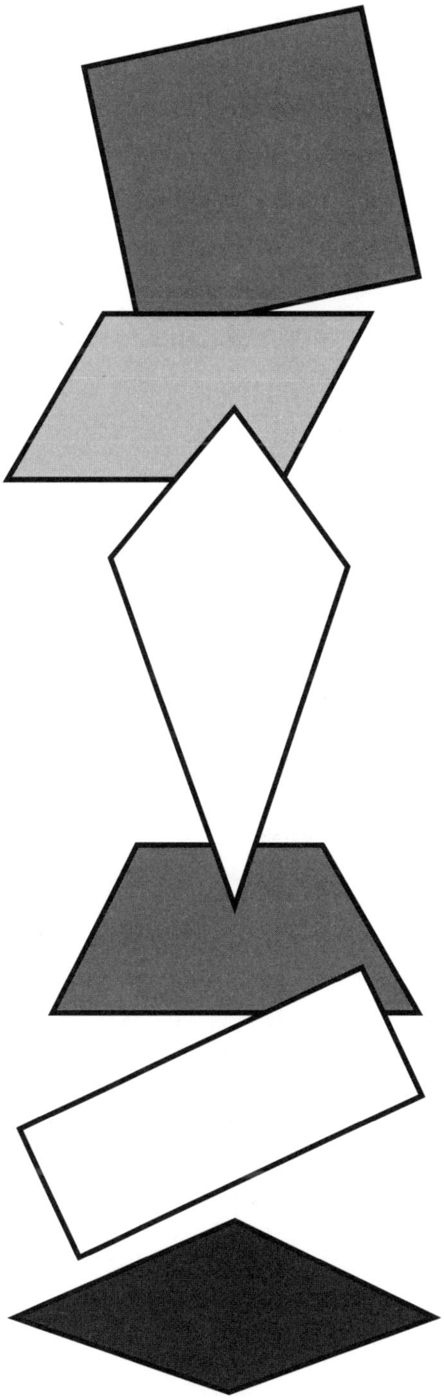

1. I have 2 pairs of parallel sides and 2 pairs of congruent angles. I have no right angles. What am I?

   ____

2. I have only one pair of parallel sides. What am I?

   ____

3. I have 2 pairs of parallel sides. All 4 of my sides are the same length, but I have no right angles. What am I?

   ____

4. I have 2 pairs of parallel sides. Each pair of sides is a different length. All 4 of my angles are right angles. What am I?

   ____

5. I have 2 pairs of touching sides the same length. None of my angles are right angles. What am I?

   ____

6. I have 2 pairs of parallel sides, and all of my sides are the same length. All of my angles have the same measure. What am I?

   ____

In Shape

Name ______________________________

Skill: Geometric shapes

Match the names with the shapes.

Plane Figures	Space Figures
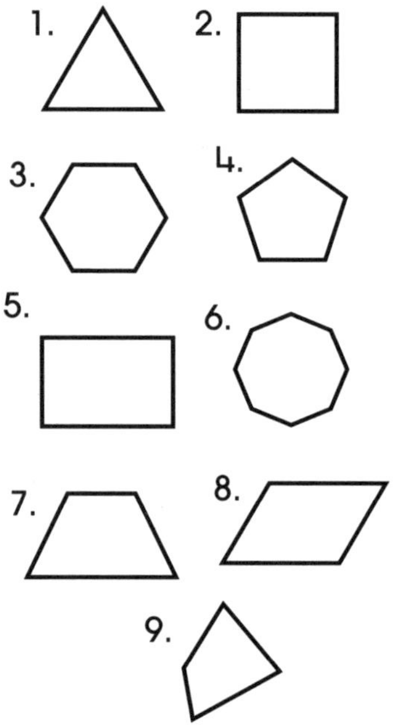	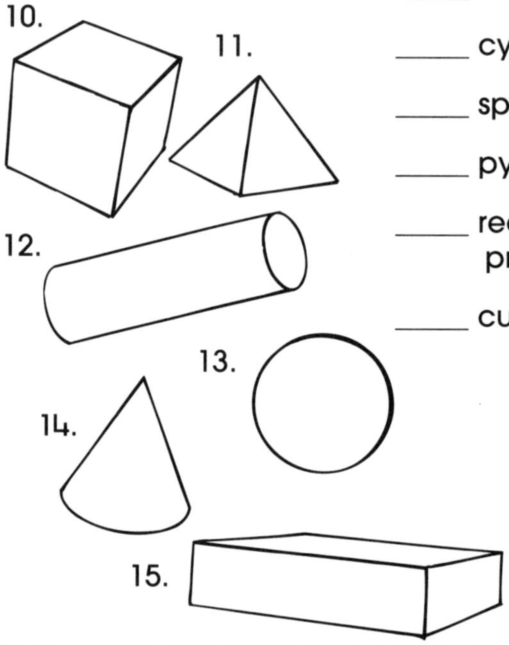
____ hexagon ____ square ____ rectangle ____ octagon ____ parallelogram ____ triangle ____ pentagon ____ trapezium ____ quadrilateral	____ cone ____ cylinder ____ sphere ____ pyramid ____ rectangular prism ____ cube

16. On a separate sheet of paper, draw a picture that contains at least one of every figure. Label the figures.

Each flat surface is a *face*. Two faces meet at an *edge*. Three (or more) edges meet at a *vertex*. Label the parts shown.

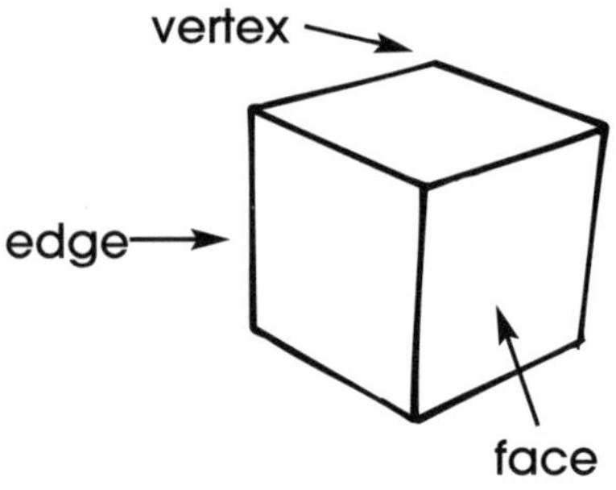

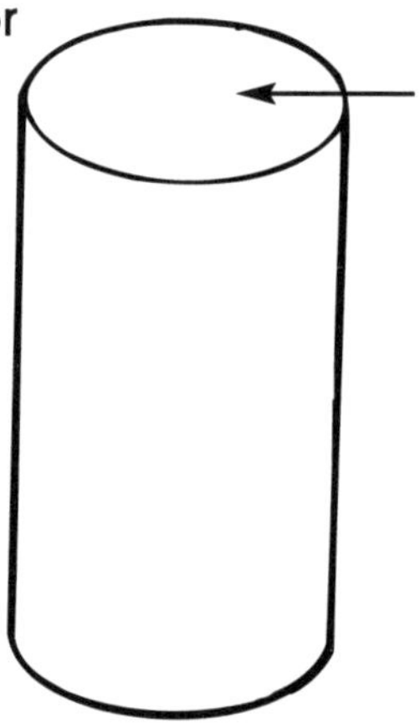

17. ____________

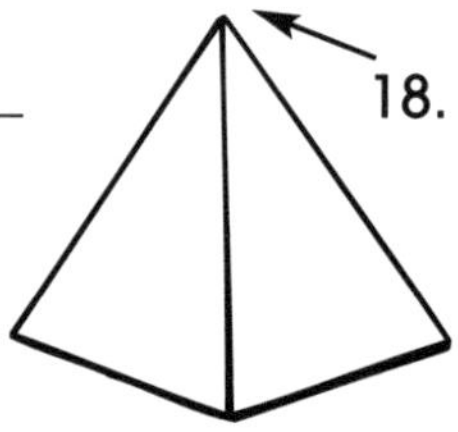

18. ____________

19. ____________

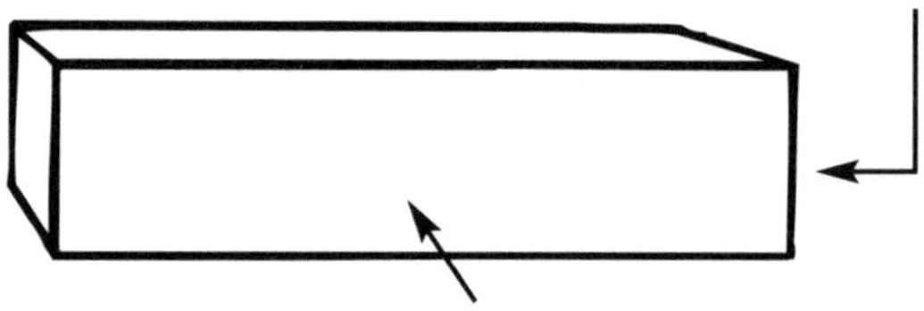

20. ____________

Write the number of sides and vertices for each figure.

21. 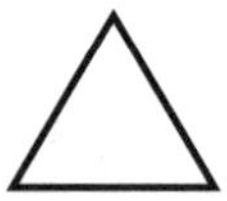 ____ sides ____ vertices

22. 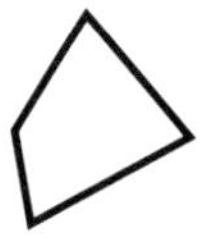 ____ sides ____ vertices

23. 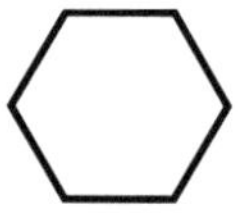 ____ sides ____ vertices

It's the Same

Skill: Congruency; symmetry; circles

Name ______________________________

A. Congruent figures have the same size and shape. Colour the congruent figures.

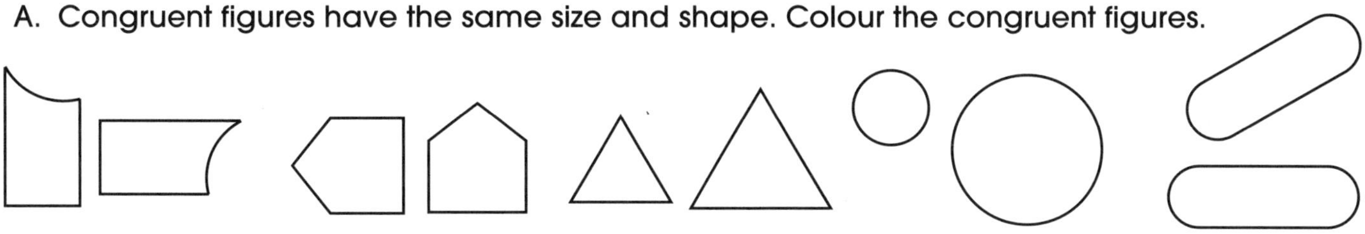

B. A line of symmetry divides a shape into congruent shapes. Colour only the figures with lines of symmetry.

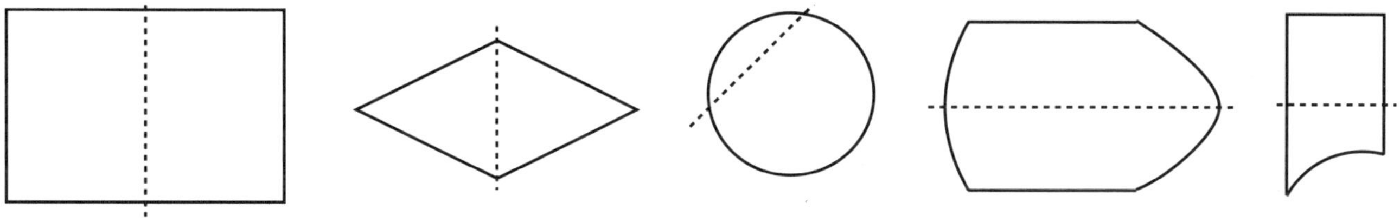

C. Use a ruler to draw two sets of congruent figures. Then draw two figures, each with a line of symmetry.

Congruent Figures	Symmetry

D.

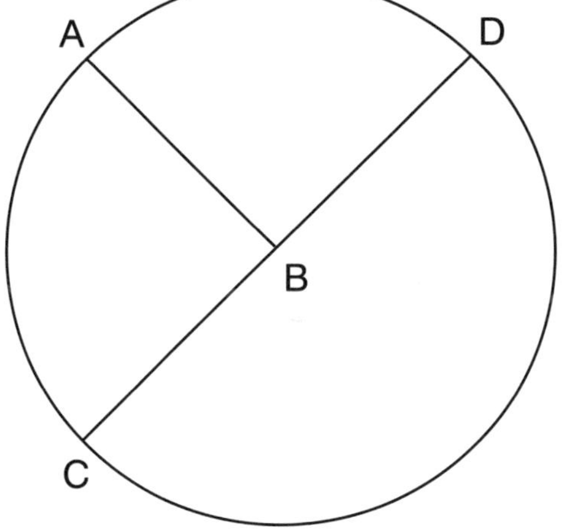

1. A circle is named by its centre.

   This circle is _______.
2. Name 2 radii. ____________
3. Name a diameter. ____________
4. Draw another diameter using a red pencil or crayon. Label it EF.
5. Draw two radii using a blue crayon. Label them BG and BH.

Congruent or Similar?

Name ______________________

Skill: Congruence and similarity

Decide if the figures below are congruent or similar.

If they are congruent, colour the figures yellow.

If they are similar, colour the figures blue.

If they are not congruent or similar, colour the figures red.

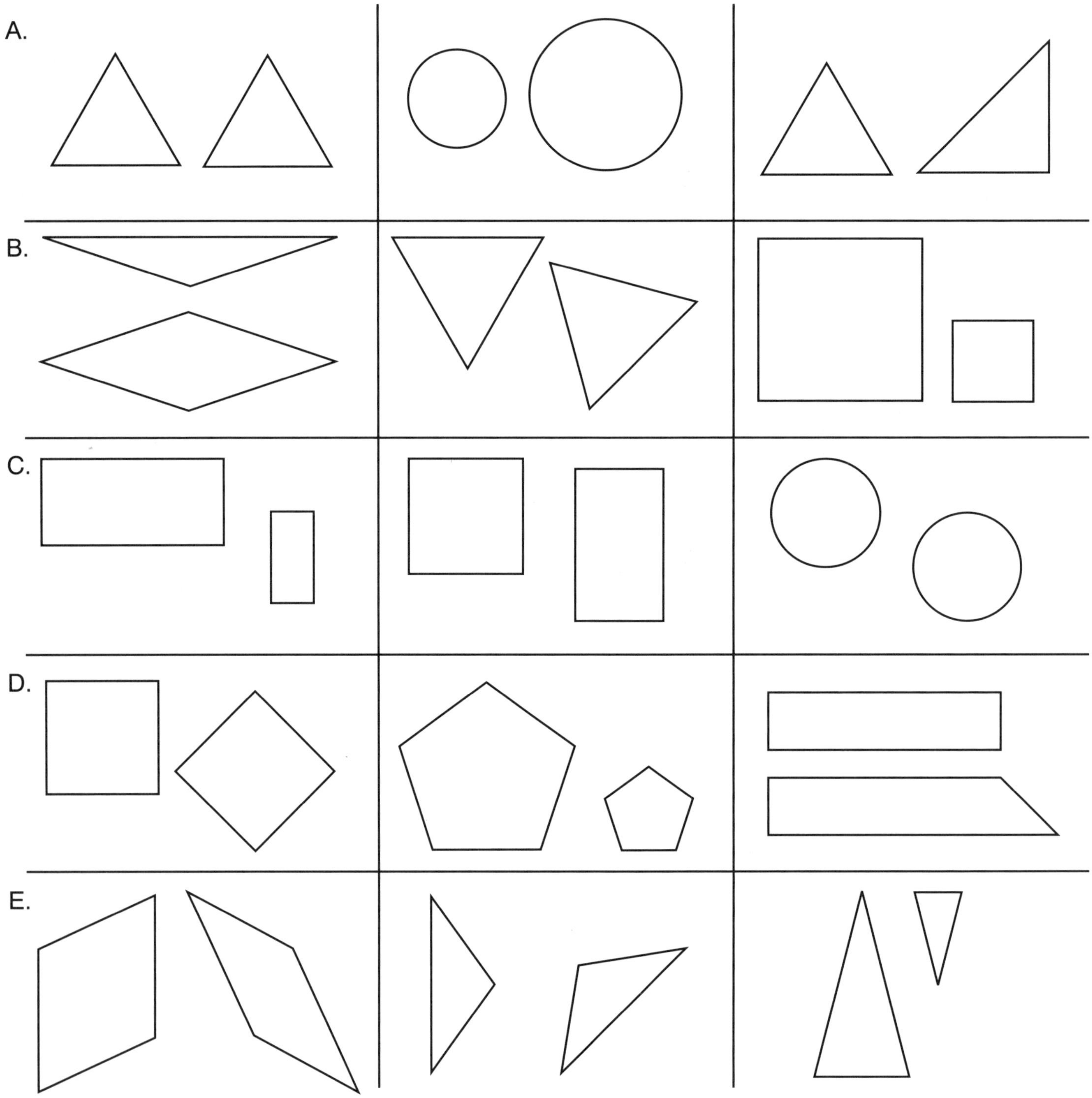

Angles and Lines

Skill: Lines and angles

Name ______________________________

Acute angles measure less than 90°.

Right angles measure 90°.

Obtuse angles measure more than 90° but less than 180°.

Parallel lines never intersect.

Perpendicular lines intersect at 90° angles.

Use the figure below to answer the questions.

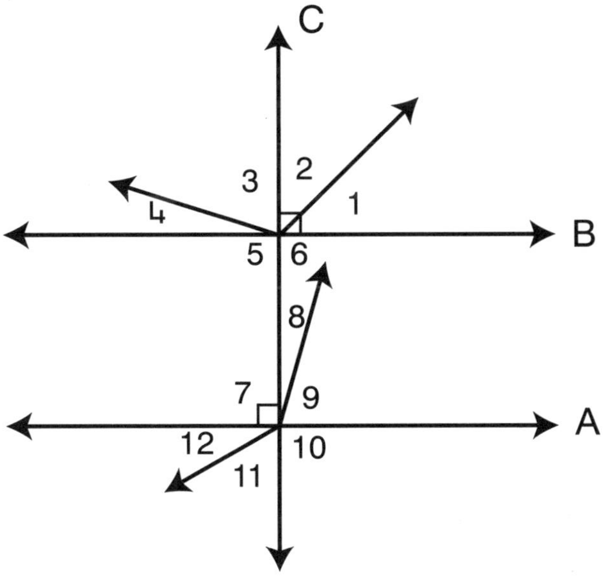

1. Name a pair of parallel lines. ______________________________
2. Name four acute angles. ______________________________
3. Name two right angles. ______________________________
4. Name a pair of perpendicular lines. ______________________________
5. Angle 11 is a(n) ______________ angle.
6. Angle 7 plus angle 8 make a(n) ______________ angle.
7. Line A is perpendicular to line ______________.
8. Angle 1 plus angle 2 make a(n) ______________ angle.
9. Draw an obtuse angle.

10. Draw a right angle.

11. Draw an acute angle.

Angling for an Answer

Name ________________________________ Skill: Measuring angles

Measure each angle. Use your answers and the code to solve the following riddle:

What is black and white and read all over?

A = 75°
A = 110°
E = 95°
E = 20°
N = 150°
P = 45°
P = 130°
R = 90°
S = 55°
W = 40°

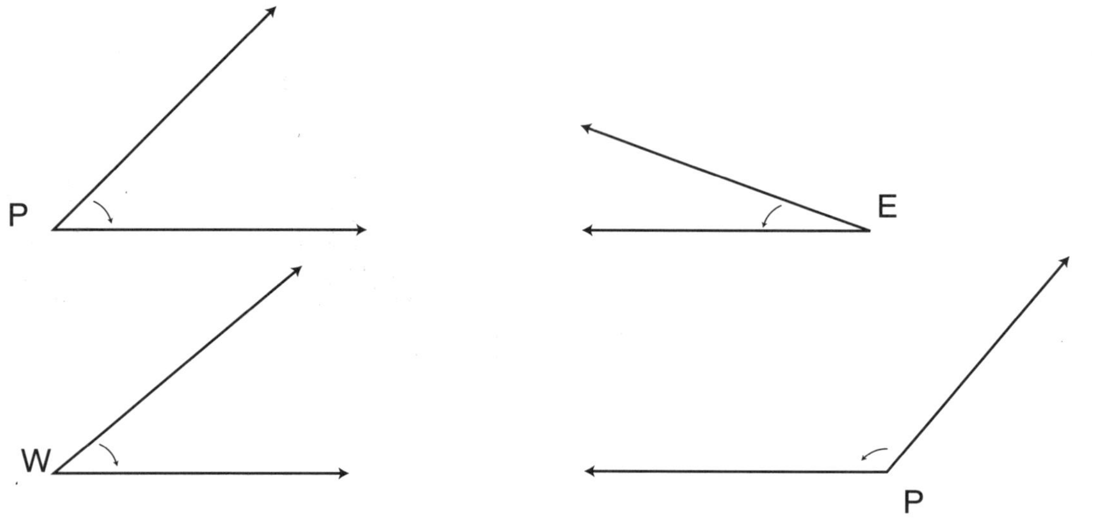

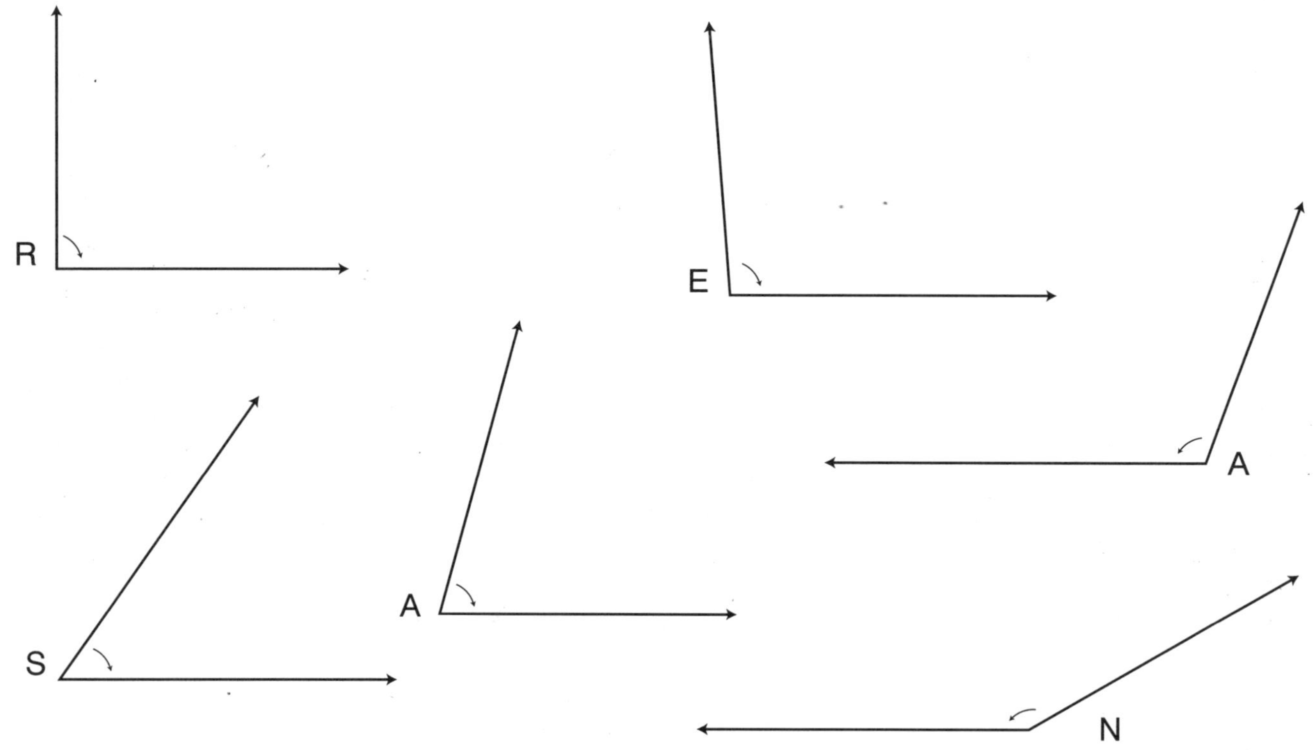

___   ___ ___ ___ ___ ___ ___ ___ ___ ___

110°   150° 20° 40° 55° 45° 75° 130° 95° 90°

Bits and Pieces

Skill: Triangles

Name ______________________________

The angles below can be combined to form four triangles. Use the letters to name each triangle.

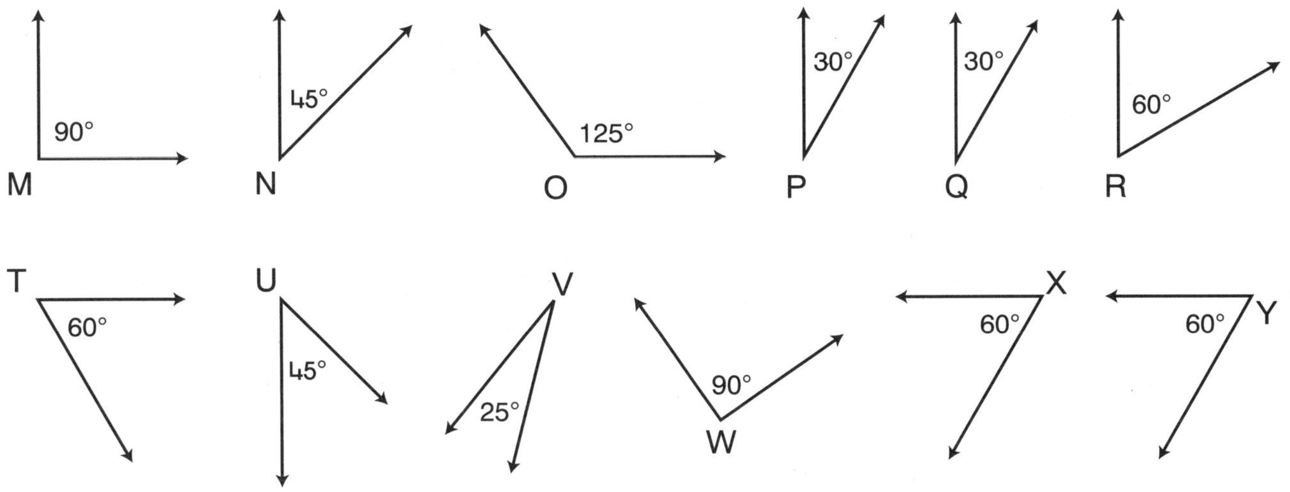

Triangle 1: ________

Triangle 2: ________

Triangle 3: ________

Triangle 4: ________

The line segments below can be combined to form triangles.
Will the triangles be scalene, isosceles, or equilateral?

Triangle 5:

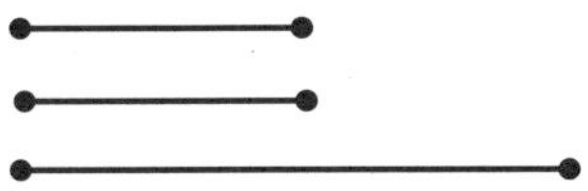

____

Triangle 6:

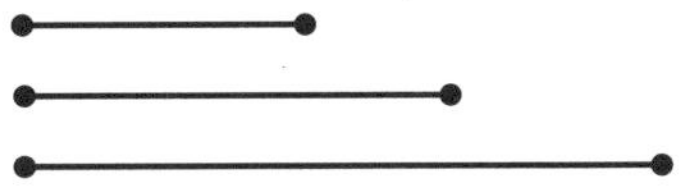

____

Triangle 7:

____

Triangle 8:

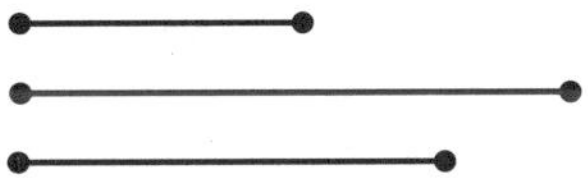

____

Triangle 9:

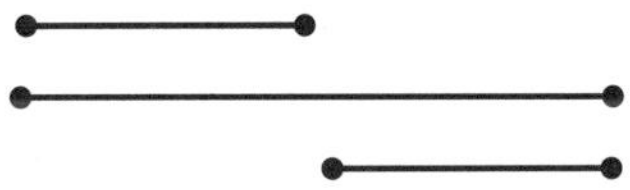

____

What's On?

Skill: Charts

Name ______________________________

You can find out many things from charts and schedules.
Read the television schedule below and answer the questions.

Saturday Morning TV Guide

Channel	6:00 a.m.	6:30 a.m.	7:00 a.m.	7:30 a.m.	8:00 a.m.	8:30 a.m.
1	Field Trip	Growing Up	Animal Fun	Puppy Pride	Cars and Trucks	Turtle Time
2	Dragon Ball	Mice From Mars	Today in Town	Fantastic Fred	Giant Spiders	Harry the Hippo
3	Nosey News	Call It	Strong Man	Wonderman	Candy	Time for Fun
4	Creature Fun	Girl Time	Adventures of Wild Warriors	Sing Me a Song		Feed the Children
5	Jellybean Jam	News Time	Masked Ranger	Tommy's Castle	Ranger Rovers	Attack of Killer Tomatoes
6				Reading for Fun	Friendly Fun	Where Is Jimmy?

1. What time does the first show start? ____________
2. What time will you need to be awake to watch "Growing Up?" ____________
   What channel is it on? ____________
3. What time will you be able to see "Adventures of Wild Warriors?" ____________
4. What show follows "Adventures of Wild Warriors" on the same channel? ________________
   How long will it last? ____________
5. What channel must you watch to learn more about reading? ____________
6. Why wouldn't you already be watching that channel? ________________________________
7. At what time do you change channels to see "Turtle Time?" ____________
   What channel is it on? ____________

Graphs, Graphs, Graphs

Name ______________________________

Skill: Line and bar graphs

There are many different ways to show information on graphs. Read each graph below and answer the questions. The temperature scale is in Fahrenheit.

This Week's Temperatures

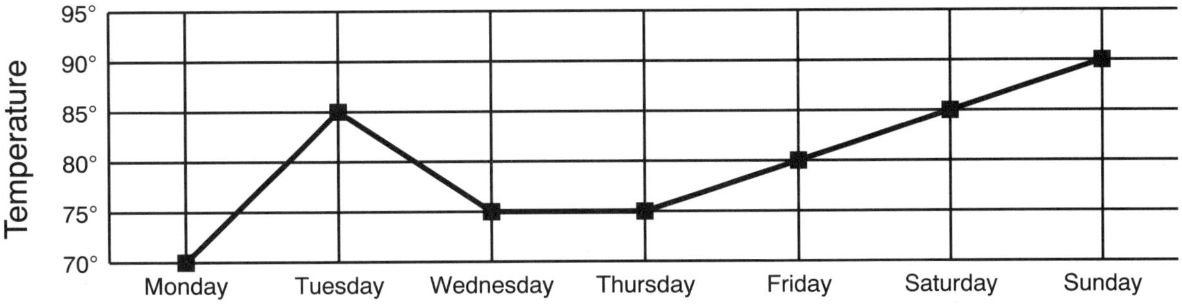

This is a ____________ graph.

1. ____________________ was the warmest day. It was _______ degrees.
2. What two days had the same cool temperature? ______________________________
3. Is the temperature rising or going down? ____________________
4. What day was the coolest day? ____________________
   What was the temperature? ___________
5. What was the difference in temperature between Monday and Sunday? ___________
6. What two days had the same warm temperature? ______________________________

How Do People Like Their Ice Cream?

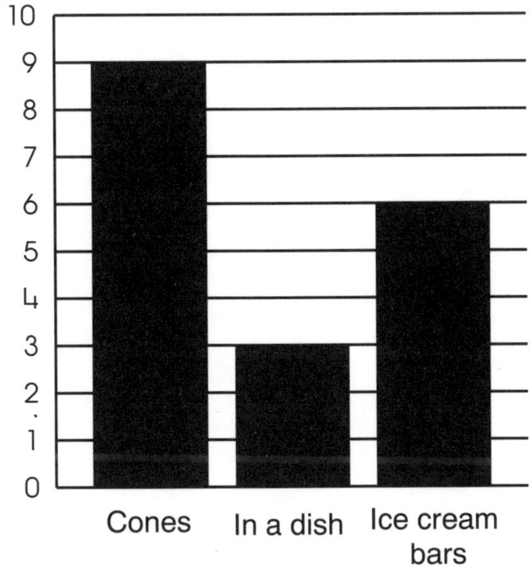

This is a ___________ graph.

7. How many more people prefer cones to bars? ___________
8. How many less people prefer a dish of ice cream than a cone? ___________
9. What do people prefer the most? ____________________
10. How many people were asked? ___________
11. How many people like cones and bars? ___________
12. How many people like a dish of ice cream and bars? ___________

Favourite Fun

Skill: Circle graphs; making graphs

Name ______________________________

Favourite Classes

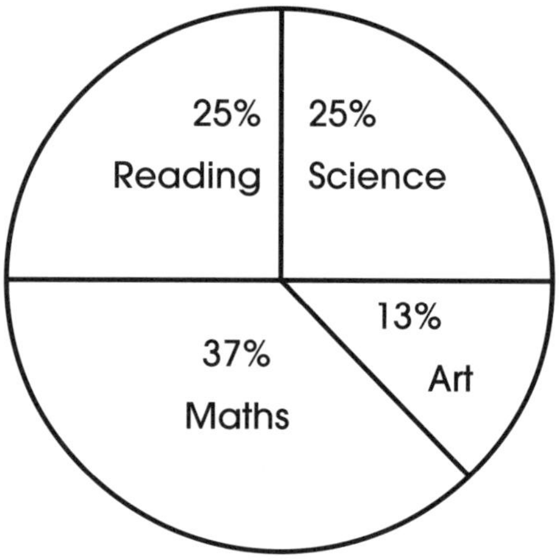

This is a ____________ graph.

Use the graph to answer the questions below. The graph represents 32 students' favourite classes.

1. What class is liked the most? ____________

   What is the percentage? ____________
2. What two classes are liked the same? ____________

   ____

   What is the percentage? ____________
3. What is the total percentage of all the classes? ______
4. What class is liked the least? ____________
5. How many students liked reading the best? ________

Make a line graph and a bar graph using the information below. Don't forget to label each side of the graphs and then give the graphs titles.

Students were asked what their favourite type of book to read was. The response was as follows:

12 liked sports.

8 liked science fiction.

10 liked history.

5 liked mystery.

5 liked riddles.

No Bones About It!

Skill: Co-ordinates graph

Name ______________________________

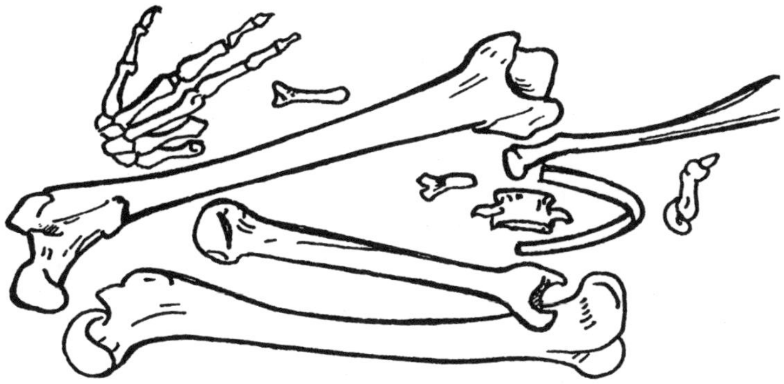

What is the largest bone in your body?

Find the points at the bottom of the page on the graph. Write the letter that represents each point above its ordered pair to find the answer to the riddle.

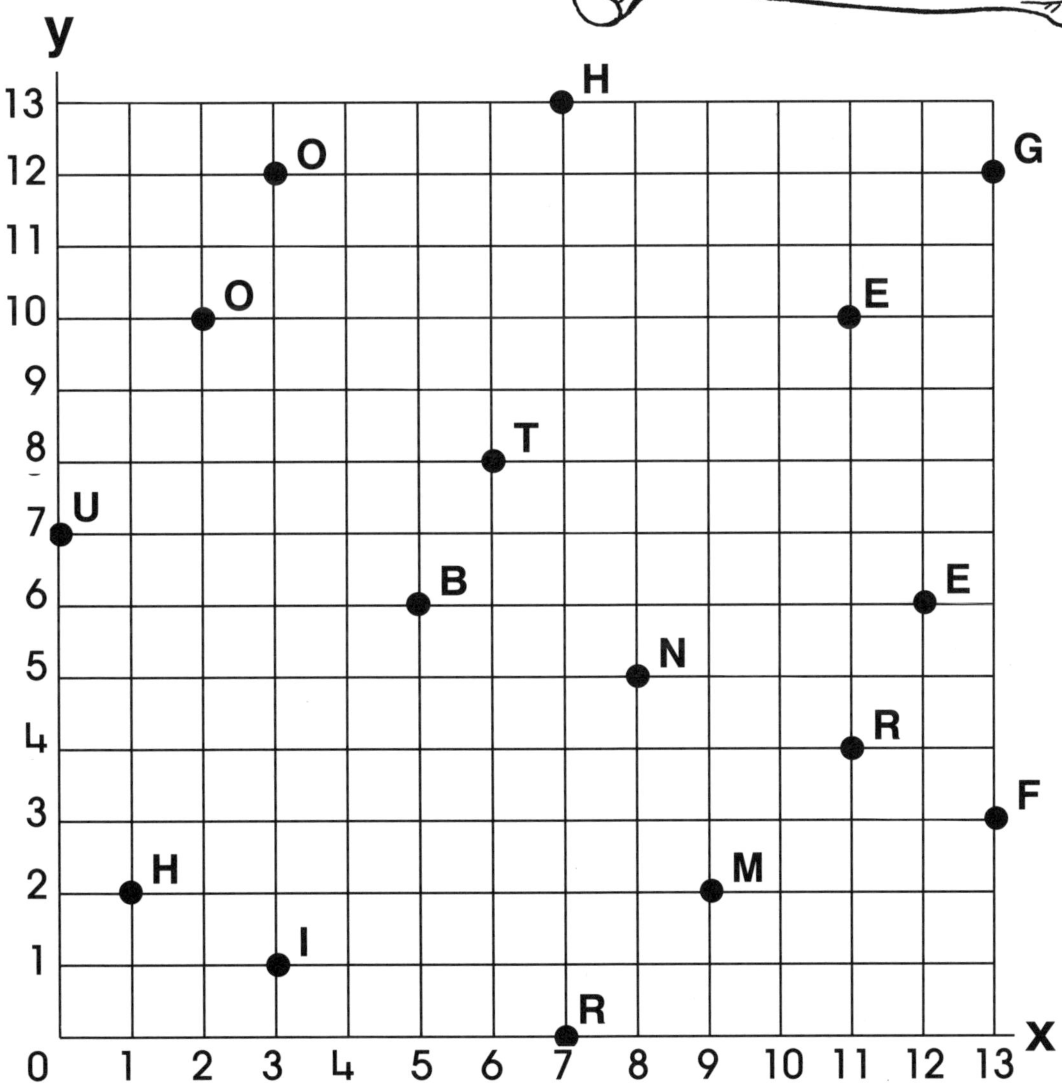

___ (6, 8) ___ (1, 2) ___ (3, 1) ___ (13, 12) ___ (7, 13)   ___ (5, 6) ___ (3, 12) ___ (8, 5) ___ (12, 6)

(___ (2, 10) ___ (11, 4)   ___ (13, 3) ___ (11, 10) ___ (9, 2) ___ (0, 7) ___ (7, 0))

Game Time

Name ______________________________

Skill: Addition key words
Addition facts 11-18

These key words are often clues that tell you to add. Use them to help you solve addition problems.

Read each problem below. Underline the key words. Then write the number sentence and the answer.

1. Four friends were playing a game. Mai counted 5 question cards. Zach counted 7. How many question cards did they count in all?

   ____

   ______ question cards

2. There are 6 bonus cards to place near "Start" and 8 bonus cards to place near the dragon. How many bonus cards are there in all?

   ____

   ______ bonus cards

3. Mai's first card let her move ahead 3 spaces. Her second card let her move ahead 9. What was the total number of spaces Mai moved?

   ____

   ______ spaces

4. Ricky's first card let him skip ahead 4 spaces. His second card let him move ahead 8. How many spaces did Ricky move altogether?

   ____

   ______ spaces

5. Zach could win if he could get an 8 and a 7 on his next two cards. What is the total number of points Zach needs to win?

   ____

   ______ points

6. Lydia won the game. She moved ahead 9 and then 7 spaces. How many spaces did she move altogether in her last two turns?

   ____

   ______ spaces

Brainwork! Write three addition word problems about a game. Use different key words in each. Ask a friend to solve them.

Too Many Pets

Name ______________________________

Skill: 2-digit subtraction

Write the number sentence and answer.

1. Mary had 26 goldfish. The cat ate 12. How many does Mary have now?

26 - 12 = 14

Mary has 14 goldfish.

2. John caught 38 lizards. 15 of them got away. How many lizards are left?

____

John has ______ lizards left.

3. Sue had 14 cats. She gave 12 of them to a friend. How many cats does Sue have now?

____

Sue has ______ cats now.

4. Jim had 29 baby hamsters. He gave 14 to a pet shop. How many does he have left?

____

Jim has ______ hamsters left.

5. Bill had 45 rabbits. He sold 25 of them. How many does he have now?

____

Bill has ______ rabbits now.

It's Your Birthday!

Name ______________________________

Skill: Comparisons 11-18

Write the number sentence and answer.

1. Ann is 11 years old. Her sister is 3. How much older is Ann than her sister?

11-3=8

8 years older.

2. John is 16 years old. Bill is 7. How much older is John than Bill?

____

______ years older.

3. Jim is 11 years old. Frank is 9. How much younger is Frank than Jim?

____

______ years younger.

4. If Mike is 14 and Nancy is 9, how much older is Mike than Nancy?

____

______ years older.

5. Jeff, who is 13 years old, has a brother who is 6. How much younger is Jeff's brother?

____

______ years younger.

Cross-Numeral Puzzle

Name ______________________________

Skill: Review

ACROSS

A. 465 + 327

F. 824 - 619

G. 700 - 215

I. 6,521 - 2,843

J. 2,774 + 984

K. 872 - 218

M. 198 + 258

N. 37 + 164

DOWN

A. 939 - 124

B. 158 + 96

C. 7,496 + 5,367

D. 8,064 + 7,296

E. 57 + 83 + 220

H. 29 + 68 + 353

L. 3,000 - 2,518

M. 219 + 212

Puzzling Problems

Name ________________________________

Skill: Dividing by 2- and 3-digit numbers

Use the clues to solve the puzzle.

ACROSS

A. 6,048 ÷ 12 = ________

C. 14,848 ÷ 16 = ________

E. 31,680 ÷ 6 = ________

G. 7,056 ÷ 84 = ________

I. 0 ÷ 36 = ________

J. 98,593 ÷ 11 = ________

M. 5,240 ÷ 10 = ________

N. 948 ÷ 12 = ________

Q. 6,630 ÷ 17 = ________

R. 6,240 ÷ 20 = ________

S. 13,000 ÷ 25 = ________

DOWN

A. 11,776 ÷ 2 = ________

B. 2,070 ÷ 46 = ________

C. 8,901 ÷ 9 = ________

D. 1,780 ÷ 89 = ________

F. 31,276 ÷ 14 = ________

H. 6,435 ÷ 13 = ________

K. 68,992 ÷ 11 = ________

L. 11,376 ÷ 3 = ________

O. 9,000 ÷ 10 = ________

P. 2,211 ÷ 67 = ________

Q. 875 ÷ 25 = ________

A		B	■	C	D	
	■	E	F			■
G	H	■			■	I
J		K		■	L	■
■	M			■	N	O
P	■		■	Q		
R			■	S		

Make a Million

Skill: Critical thinking

Name ______________________________

Complete each problem so that the sum is one million.

A.

237,512	456,897	79,936	______
+ ______	+ ______	+ ______	+ 384,207
1,000,000	1,000,000	1,000,000	1,000,000

B.

564,216	935,142	______	499,999
+ ______	+ ______	+ 99,384	+ ______
1,000,000	1,000,000	1,000,000	1,000,000

C.

424,116	______	82,936	496,385
______	384,109	426,817	______
+ 61,532	+ 123,816	+ ______	+ 216,419
1,000,000	1,000,000	1,000,000	1,000,000

D.

369,804	______	831,678	23,182
______	664,819	______	976,596
+ 566,157	+ 309,662	+ 29,814	+ ______
1,000,000	1,000,000	1,000,000	1,000,000

Write two problems of your own that have sums of one million.

E.

______
+ ______
1,000,000

F.

______
+ ______
1,000,000

Run for Fun and Fitness

Name ______________________

Skill: Problem solving with fractions

Anna and Robyn run every day. They record their distances in a table.

Running Log (in miles)

Day	Monday	Tuesday	Wednesday	Thursday	Friday
Anna	$3\,^{1}/_{2}$	$4\,^{3}/_{4}$	$3\,^{1}/_{2}$	5	$5\,^{3}/_{4}$
Robyn	$3\,^{7}/_{8}$	4	$4\,^{1}/_{4}$	$4\,^{7}/_{8}$	$5\,^{5}/_{8}$

Solve. Write addition or subtraction equations to help you.

1. How far did Anna run on Monday and Tuesday? __________
2. How far did Robyn run on Wednesday and Thursday? __________
3. On which day was Robyn and Anna's combined distance least? greatest?

____

4. Who ran further on Monday? By how many miles?

____

5. Who ran further on Thursday? By how many miles?

____

6. Estimate the total number of miles run by each runner for the five-day period.

____

7. On which day did Anna and Robyn run a total of about 10 miles?

____

8. On which day did Robyn run more than $^{1}/_{2}$ mile farther than Anna?

____

Super Sentences

Name ______________________________

Skill: Adding fractions with unlike denominators

Complete the number sentences below. Simplify all answers.

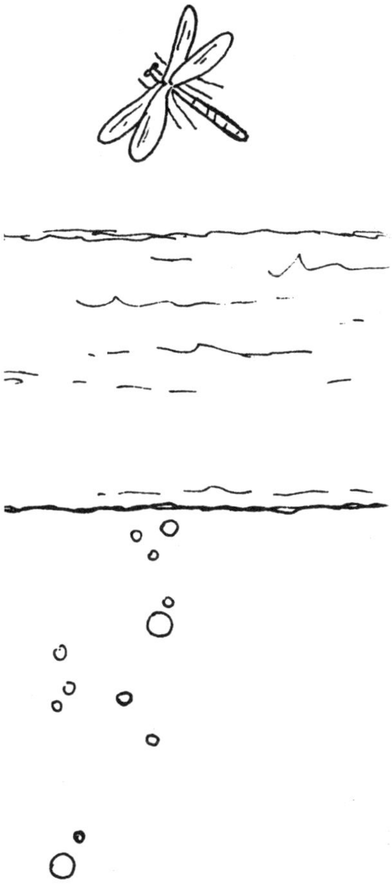

$\frac{2}{3}$	+	$\frac{14}{15}$	=	
+		+		
$\frac{1}{30}$	+	$\frac{1}{6}$	=	
=		=		+
				$\frac{1}{40}$
				=
$\frac{1}{8}$	+	$\frac{1}{10}$	=	
+		+		
$\frac{1}{4}$	+	$\frac{1}{5}$	=	
=		=		+
	+		=	
				=

Puzzling Problems

Skill: Percentage of a number

Name ______________________________

Find the percent problems. Use your answers to solve the puzzle.

ACROSS

A. 10% of 100 = ______
B. 20% of 125 = ______
D. 33 1/3% of 135 = ______
E. 66 2/3% of 75 = ______
F. 50% of 130 = ______
G. 15% of 500 = ______
H. 5% of 16,000 = ______
I. 25% of 360 = ______
J. 10% of 150 = ______
L. 20% of 150 = ______
M. 50% of 90 = ______
N. 50% of 1,120 = ______
P. 25% of 280 = ______
Q. 50% of 160 = ______
R. 20% of 450 = ______

DOWN

A. 20% of 75 = ______
B. 40% of 50 = ______
C. 50% of 750 = ______
D. 5% of 8,000 = ______
E. 10% of 550 = ______
F. 25% of 2,500 = ______
G. 66 2/3% of 105 = ______
H. 50% of 170 = ______
I. 25% of 380 = ______
J. 1% of 10,000 = ______
K. 50% of 450 = ______
L. 25% of 140 = ______
M. 80% of 50 = ______
O. 80% of 750 = ______
P. 50% of 140 = ______
Q. 25% of 340 = ______

Euler's Law

Name ________________________

Skill: Faces, edges and vertices

Complete the table to learn about Euler's Law.

Space Figure	Vertices	Faces	Sum of vertices and faces	Edges
1. 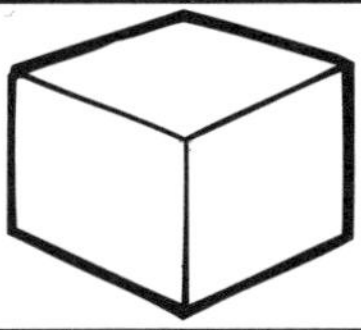				
2. 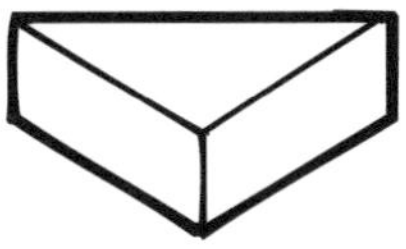				
3. 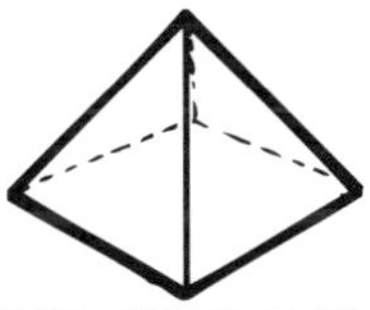				
4. 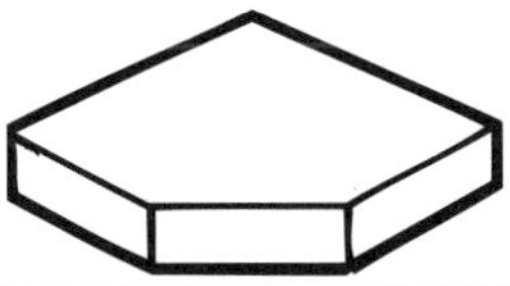				
5. 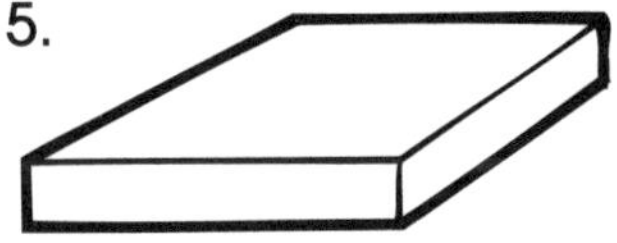				
6. 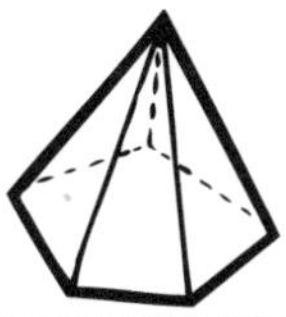				
7. 				

What do you notice about the sum of the faces and vertices and the number of edges in each figure?

____

____

Answer Key

Millions and Millions

Name ______________________ Skill: Place value - millions

Write each number in the place value boxes.

	Millions			Thousands			Ones		
1. 65,703,516		6	5	7	0	3	5	1	6
2. 841,654,812	8	4	1	6	5	4	8	1	2
3. 140,372,166	1	4	0	3	7	2	1	6	6

Write the numbers.

4. five million, seven hundred thousand, nine hundred and two
5.700.902
5. 20,000,000 + 50,000 + 7,000 + 600 + 80 + 4
20.057.684
6. one million, nine hundred and six thousand, two hundred and six
1.906.206
7. 2,000,000 + 600,000 + 40,000 + 300 + 20 + 1
2.640.321
8. nine million, two hundred and two thousand
9.202.000
9. twenty-five million, eight hundred and one
25,000,801
10. 19,000,000 + 50,000 + 900 + 5
19,050,905
11. 400,000,000 + 3,000,000 + 90,000 + 70 + 7
403,090,077
12. seventeen million, sixty-four thousand, and ninety-six
17,064,096

Page 1

Big Fish

Name ______________________ Skill: Place value - millions

Write the numbers in the puzzle.

Across

1. eight hundred and eighty-nine thousand, six hundred and twelve
6. forty-three thousand and eleven
8. eight thousand, four hundred and forty
9. three hundred million, eight hundred and sixty-five thousand, seven hundred and seventy-two
10. thirty-nine thousand and thirteen
11. six thousand, five hundred and eighty-eight
14. forty million, two thousand, one hundred and sixty-two
16. thirty thousand, one hundred and nine
18. five hundred and fifty thousand, one hundred and twenty-three
19. fifty thousand, seven hundred and eighty-six

Write the word name for each number.

Down

2. eight hundred and twenty one million, eight hundred and thirty seven thousand and ten
3. thirteen thousand, nine hundred and eighty-six
4. one million, one hundred and forty five thousand, five hundred and three
5. two million, three hundred and nine thousand, six hundred and forty nine.
7. one hundred and seventy eight thousand and thirty two
12. eight million, five hundred and ten thousand, five hundred and thirty seven
13. eight hundred and nineteen thousand and one
15. twenty five thousand and eighty one
17. seventy two thousand, one hundred and twenty three.

Page 2

Let's Compare

Name ______________________ Skill: Comparing numbers

Write > or <.

A.	10,769 (<) 11,200	177,204 (>) 116,791	97,213 (<) 107,213
B.	86,190 (>) 84,993	981,203 (>) 918,203	72,218 (<) 75,003
C.	198,221 (>) 98,221	264,193 (<) 266,001	83,103 (>) 80,793
D.	656,183 (<) 665,183	199,820 (>) 198,993	55,186 (>) 54,939

E. Write the numbers in order in the chart below.

756,802	694,213	820,000	971,246	378,461	192,874
471,622	216,606	92,813	87,214	63,744	55,806

Big	Bigger	Biggest
1. 55,806	5. 192,874	9. 694,213
2. 63,744	6. 216,606	10. 756,802
3. 87,214	7. 378,461	11. 820,000
4. 92,813	8. 471,622	12. 971,246

F. The smallest number is 55,806.
The largest number is 971,246.

G. Write the number that is 10 less than the smallest number. 55,796
Write the number that is 100 more than the smallest number. 55,906
Write the number that is 1000 more than the largest number. 972,246

Page 3

Round and Round

Name ______________________ Skill: Rounding numbers

Round each number to the nearest 10, 100 or 1000.

A. 10		B. 100		C. 1000	
85	90	467	500	5,764	6,000
47	50	821	800	8,213	8,000
293	290	299	300	9,621	10,000
64	60	1,371	1,400	2,473	2,000
327	330	5,614	5,600	1,121	1,000

D. Round to the nearest thousand. Colour the balls when the numbers round up.

1. 4,651 – 5,000
2. 9,961 – 10,000
3. 7,208 – 7,000
4. 2,976 – 3,000
5. 899 – 1,000
6. 3,479 – 3,000
7. 6,411 – 6,000
8. 5,743 – 6,000
9. 1,372 – 1,000
10. 4,493 – 4,000
11. 7,510 – 8,000
12. 6,821 – 7,000
13. 2,093 – 2,000
14. 4,499 – 4,000
15. 8,803 – 9,000

E. Answers for tens need to end in one zero(s).
Those for the nearest hundred end in two zero(s).
Answers to the nearest thousand end in three zero(s).

Page 4

Answer Key

The Highest Peak

Name ______________________ Skill: Highest common factor

Find the highest common factor (HCF) for each pair of numbers. Then cross out one square at the bottom of the page that contains the answer. The letters to the remaining squares, written in order, will spell the answer to the following question:

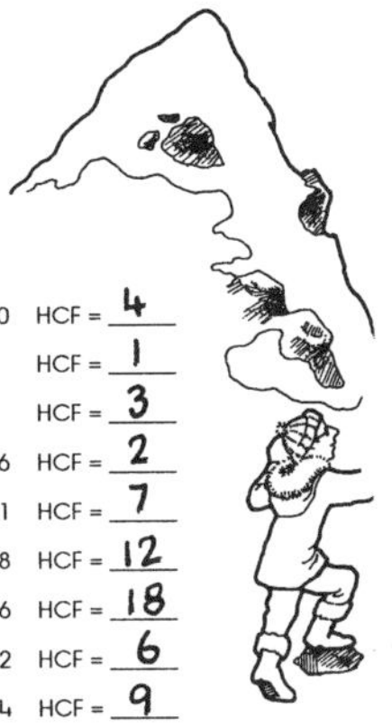

What is the highest mountain peak in the world?

A.	12 and 30	HCF = 6	16 and 20	HCF = 4
B.	8 and 10	HCF = 2	7 and 9	HCF = 1
C.	6 and 12	HCF = 6	9 and 12	HCF = 3
D.	21 and 35	HCF = 7	10 and 16	HCF = 2
E.	12 and 18	HCF = 6	14 and 21	HCF = 7
F.	15 and 40	HCF = 5	36 and 48	HCF = 12
G.	16 and 24	HCF = 8	18 and 36	HCF = 18
H.	21 and 45	HCF = 3	24 and 42	HCF = 6
I.	18 and 30	HCF = 6	45 and 54	HCF = 9
J.	22 and 52	HCF = 2	16 and 64	HCF = 16

M 0	A 6	C 6	O 30	J 2	H 2	U 11	L 12
P 8	N 15	Q 6	B 7	T 10	H 6	Y 6	E 13
Z 18	U 7	V 22	G 3	X 1	E 20	R 14	K 6
F 2	E 17	W 6	S 21	C 9	I 2	D 16	T 25

MOUNT EVEREST

Page 5

"Just About" Answers

Name ______________________ Skill: Estimating sums and differences

Use rounding to estimate each sum or difference below. Then shade a section in the box at the bottom of the page that matches your answer to find a secret word.

A. 28 + 92 = 120; 73 + 68 = 140; 133 − 67 = 60; 166 − 78 = 90; 617 + 376 = 1,000

B. 44 + 59 = 100; 1,486 − 626 = 900; 681 − 324 = 400; 6,790 + 3,456 = 10,000; 15,897 − 8,584 = 7,000

C. 368 + 429 = 800; 1,295 − 787 = 500; 1,869 − 451 = 1,400; 1,303 − 698 = 600; 17,498 − 8,329 = 9,000

D. 12,645 − 9,103 = 4,000; 698 − 462 = 200; 2,375 + 2,814 = 5,000; 1,014 + 5,321 = 6,000; 8,247 + 9,983 = 18,000

120	7,000	400	3,000	1,000	19,000	
4,000	300	140	8,000	1,400	9,000	15,000
800	700	5,000	11,000	18,000	14,000	17,000
200	2,000	90	12,000	6,000	10,000	20,000
600	60	500	16,000	100	13,000	900

What's the secret word? OK

Page 6

"Sum Difference"

Name ______________________ Skill: Estimating sums and differences

Estimate each sum or difference by rounding each number to the nearest hundred. Add or subtract. Shade in the boxes that have answers of 500 or more.

1. 927 − 419 → 900 − 400	2. 841 + 219 → 800 + 200 = 1000	3. 164 + 99 → 200 + 100 = 300	4. 617 − 302 → 600 − 300 = 300
5. 897 − 143 → 900 − 100 = 800	6. 222 + 170 → 200 + 200 = 400	7. 719 − 504 → 700 − 500 = 200	8. 921 − 647 → 900 − 600 = 300
9. 302 + 256 → 300 + 300 = 600	10. 392 + 184 → 400 + 200 = 600	11. 621 − 304 → 600 − 300 = 300	12. 640 + 599 → 600 + 600 = 1200
13. 163 + 173 → 200 + 200 = 400	14. 610 − 601 → 600 − 600 = 0	15. 707 − 290 → 700 − 300 = 400	16. 701 + 291 → 700 + 300 = 1000
17. 816 + 219 → 800 + 200 = 1000	18. 999 − 702 → 1000 − 700 = 300	19. 797 − 142 → 800 − 100 = 700	20. 146 + 208 → 100 + 200 = 300
21. 504 − 392 → 500 − 400 = 100	22. 109 + 99 → 100 + 100 = 200	23. 697 − 64 → 700 − 100 = 600	24. 299 − 199 → 300 − 200 = 100

Page 7

Another Kind of Number

Name ______________________ Skill: Roman numerals

A. Finish the chart.

I = 1	VII = 7	XL = 40	C = 100	DC = 600
II = 2	VIII = 8	L = 50	CC = 200	DCC = 700
III = 3	IX = 9	LX = 60	CCC = 300	DCCL = 750
IV = 4	X = 10	LXX = 70	CCCL = 350	DCCC = 800
V = 5	XX = 20	LXXX = 80	CD = 400	CM = 900
VI = 6	XXX = 30	XC = 90	D = 500	M = 1,000

B. To make the numbers between 10–13, add ones (I) to ten (X).

Write 11, 12, and 13 in Roman numerals. 11 = XI 12 = XII 13 = XIII

Fifteen is 10 + 5, or XV.

For 16, 17, and 18, add ones to 15. 16 = XVI 17 = XVII 18 = XVIII

For 14, subtract 1 from 15 by putting the one in front of 5. 14 = XIV

For 19, subtract 1 from 20 by putting the one in front of the second 10. 19 = XIX

C. Following the rules above, write the numbers.

XXII = 22 XXXIII = 33 LII = 52 CDXCI = 491

CL = 150 CLX = 160 DL = 550 DCLI = 651

D. Draw lines to match.

CCCX	560	XVI	24
XXXIV	8	CCXC	16
DLX	310	DX	19
VIII	34	XIX	290
XIV	805	XXIV	510
DCCCV	14	MMCIX	740
MIX	1,009	DCCXL	2,109

Page 8

Answer Key

Riddle

Skill: 2-and 3-digit addends, regrouping

Name ____________________

Riddle: The answer is a walkie-talkie.

But I don't think it's possible.

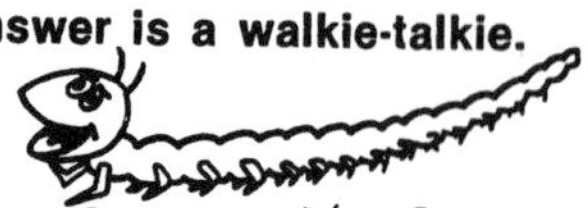

W H A T — 511 455 534 850; D O — 163 954; Y O u — 886 954

G E T — 660 730 850; W H E N — 511 455 730 571; Y O u — 886 954

C R O S S — 843 838 954 980 980; A — 534

C E N T I P E D E — 843 730 571 850 973 397 730 163 730

W I T H — 511 973 850 455; A — 534; R A D I O? — 838 534 163 973 954

A: 418 + 116 = 534	C: 724 + 119 = 843	D: 128 + 35 = 163	E: 414 + 316 = 730	G: 25 + 635 = 660
H: 39 + 416 = 455	I: 349 + 624 = 973	N: 524 + 47 = 571	O: 427 + 527 = 954	P: 289 + 108 = 397
R: 519 + 319 = 838	S: 127 + 853 = 980	T: 811 + 39 = 850	W: 28 + 483 = 511	Y: 327 + 559 = 886

Page 9

A Happy Thought

Skill: 2-and 3-digit addends, regrouping

Name ____________________

Are you out there?

H E L L O — 858 576 973 973 442; T O — 634 442; A L L — 150 973 973

T H E — 634 858 576; F R I E N D S — 662 790 371 576 357 83 732

I'V E — 371 638 576; Y E T — 972 576 634; T O — 634 442

M E E T! — 64 576 576 634

A: 113 + 37 = 150	D: 46 + 37 = 83	E: 529 + 47 = 576	F: 18 + 644 = 662	H: 29 + 829 = 858
I: 126 + 245 = 371	L: 427 + 546 = 973	M: 29 + 35 = 64	N: 109 + 248 = 357	O: 228 + 214 = 442
R: 447 + 343 = 790	S: 416 + 316 = 732	T: 419 + 215 = 634	V: 219 + 419 = 638	Y: 143 + 829 = 972

Page 10

Tongue Twister

Skill: 2-and 3-digit addends, regrouping

Name ____________________

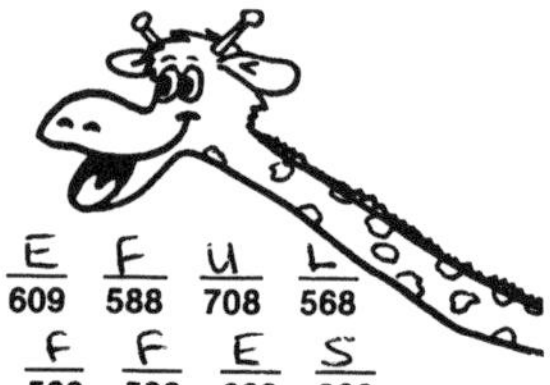

G R A C E F U L — 924 647 450 406 609 588 708 568

G I R A F F E S — 924 616 647 450 588 588 609 938

G R A Z E — 924 647 450 306 609; O N — 576 227

G I G A N T I C — 924 616 924 450 227 840 616 406

G R A P E S. — 924 647 450 829 609 938

A: 260 + 190 = 450	C: 150 + 256 = 406	E: 532 + 77 = 609	F: 397 + 191 = 588	G: 462 + 462 = 924
I: 240 + 376 = 616	L: 287 + 281 = 568	N: 173 + 54 = 227	O: 386 + 190 = 576	P: 648 + 181 = 829
R: 573 + 74 = 647	S: 767 + 171 = 938	T: 450 + 390 = 840	U: 346 + 362 = 708	Z: 113 + 193 = 306

Page 11

A Tongue Twister

Skill: 3-digit addends, no regrouping

Name ____________________

S E V E N — 698 587 339 587 739; S I L V E R — 698 949 483 339 587 509

S N A K E S — 698 739 357 799 587 698

S L I T H E R E D — 698 483 949 228 448 587 509 587 444

S L O W L y — 698 483 299 593 483

S O U T H W A R D. — 698 299 559 228 448 593 357 509 444

A: 234 + 123 = 357	D: 221 + 223 = 444	E: 233 + 354 = 587	H: 320 + 128 = 448	I: 713 + 236 = 949
K: 308 + 491 = 799	L: 300 + 183 = 483	N: 524 + 215 = 739	O: 128 + 171 = 299	R: 406 + 103 = 509
S: 495 + 203 = 698	T: 125 + 103 = 228	U: 328 + 231 = 559	V: 216 + 123 = 339	W: 272 + 321 = 593

Page 12

Answer Key

A Tongue Twister

Skill: 3-digit addends, regrouping

Name ____________________

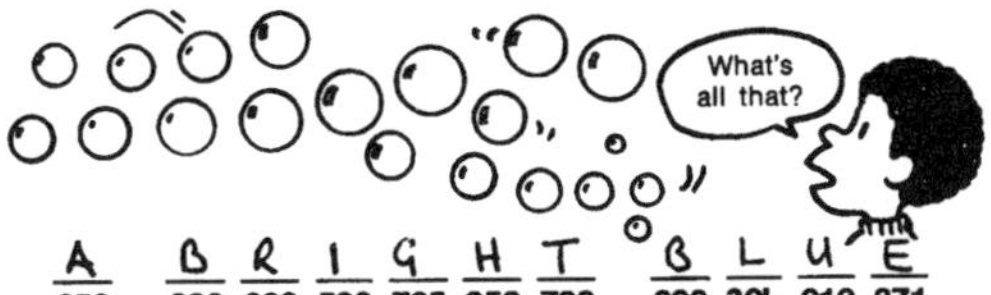

A BRIGHT BLUE
652 890 666 593 785 950 793 890 394 212 371

BRONTOSAURUS
890 666 991 874 793 991 442 652 212 666 212 442

BLEW BILLIONS
890 394 371 910 890 593 394 394 593 991 874 442

OF BROWN
991 668 890 666 991 910 874

BUBBLES.
890 212 890 890 394 371 442

A 436 + 216 = 652	B 771 + 119 = 890	E 157 + 214 = 371	F 529 + 139 = 668	G 358 + 427 = 785
H 845 + 105 = 950	I 164 + 429 = 593	L 207 + 187 = 394	N 525 + 349 = 874	O 185 + 806 = 991
R 538 + 128 = 666	S 223 + 219 = 442	T 558 + 235 = 793	U 109 + 103 = 212	W 705 + 205 = 910

Page 13

A Riddle

Skill: 3-digit addends, regrouping

Name ____________________

Riddle: Why do monsters forget?

EVERYTHING
929 612 929 944 534 627 695 988 934 867

GOES IN ONE
867 504 929 643 988 934 504 934 929

EAR AND
929 807 944 807 934 339

OUT THE
504 510 627 627 695 929

OTHERS IX.
504 627 695 929 944 643 988 745

A 343 + 464 = 807	D 166 + 173 = 339	E 299 + 630 = 929	G 585 + 282 = 867	H 541 + 154 = 695
I 293 + 695 = 988	N 583 + 351 = 934	O 292 + 212 = 504	R 793 + 151 = 944	S 350 + 293 = 643
T 493 + 134 = 627	U 130 + 380 = 510	V 351 + 261 = 612	X 453 + 292 = 745	Y 343 + 191 = 534

Page 14

Adding Larger Numbers

Name ____________________

Skill: 4-digit addition

A.	2,714 + 3,281 = 5995	4,265 + 5,135 = 9,400	6,223 + 290 = 6,513	2,227 + 1,462 = 3,689	5,540 + 1,628 = 7,168
B.	4,175 + 377 = 4,552	1,097 + 1,983 = 3,080	7,142 + 2,355 = 9,497	8,426 + 722 = 9,148	1,014 + 792 = 1,806
C.	6,514 + 1,922 = 8,436	3,555 + 1,671 = 5,226	892 + 3,419 = 4,311	5,001 + 4,232 = 9,233	1,660 + 2,237 = 3,897
D.	1,554 + 667 = 2,221	8,817 + 1,012 = 9,829	5,572 + 918 = 6,490	1,090 + 703 = 1,793	2,813 + 2,763 = 5,576
E.	4,272 + 624 = 4,896	1,456 + 1,417 = 2,873	5,915 + 1,775 = 7,690	1,500 + 1,458 = 2,958	7,254 + 746 = 8000
F.	2,754 + 2,787 = 5,541	2,861 + 668 = 3,529	7,565 + 1,907 = 9,472	4,841 + 1,827 = 6,668	5,817 + 2,062 = 7,879
G.	1,533 + 1,316 = 2,849	2,376 + 1,849 = 4,225	4,458 + 998 = 5,456	8,814 + 1,092 = 9,906	3,464 + 3,721 = 7,185

Page 15

Shapely Sums

Skill: 4-digit addition

Name ____________________

Working diagonally, add the numbers shown by the arrows.
Write >, <, or = to compare the sums.

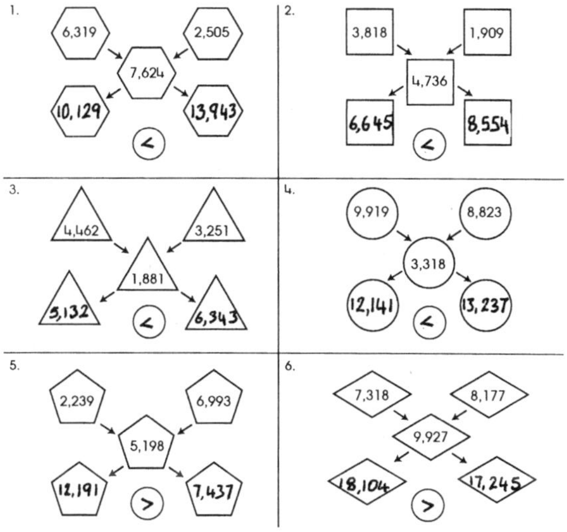

Write the name of the shape in each puzzle.

1. hexagon 2. square 3. triangle
4. circle 5. pentagon 6. rhombus

Page 16

Answer Key

Flower Problems

Skill: Subtracting multiples of 10

Name ______________________

Score 40

Write the answers in the petals.

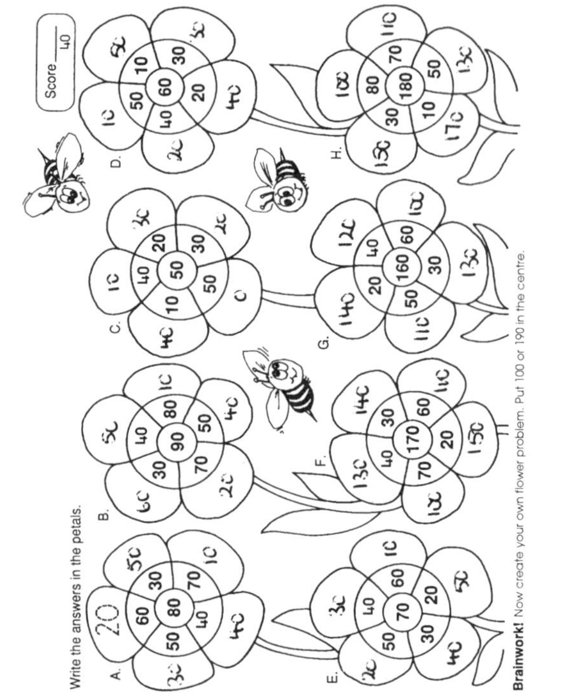

Brainwork! Now create your own flower problem. Put 100 or 190 in the centre.

Copyright © 1999 Brighter Vision Education Ltd 17 Maths, KS2

Page 17

Taking a Bite

Skill: 2-digit subtraction, regrouping

Name ______________________

Score 35

Subtract and write the answers. To find where the worm bit the apple, colour the box with the greatest answer.

A.	24 − 13 = 11	86 − 52 = 34	89 − 36 = 53	77 − 5 = 72		
B.	57 − 22 = 35	19 − 5 = 14	68 − 24 = 44	71 − 50 = 21	86 − 13 = 73	50 − 10 = 40
C.	69 − 23 = 46	88 − 12 = 76	45 − 13 = 32	28 − 12 = 16	94 − 24 = 70	76 − 73 = 3
D.	52 − 10 = 42	79 − 61 = 33	49 − 22 = 27	70 − 40 = 30	95 − 4 = 91	87 − 12 = 75
E.	79 − 70 = 9	39 − 11 = 28	36 − 32 = 4	28 − 2 = 26	99 − 55 = 44	98 − 15 = 83
F.		77 − 45 = 32	68 − 20 = 48	49 − 32 = 17	87 − 30 = 57	
G.		88 − 72 = 16	76 − 21 = 55	99 − 68 = 31		

Copyright © 1999 Brighter Vision Education Ltd 18 Maths, KS2

Page 18

Space Walk

Skill: 2-digit subtraction, regrouping

Name ______________________

34 — Yellow
35 — Orange
36 — Brown
37 — Blue

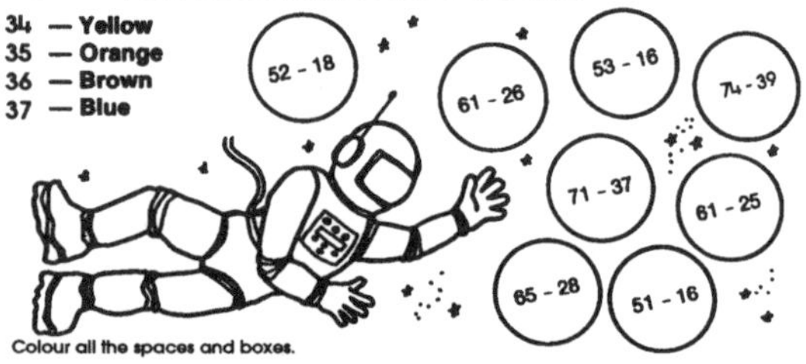

Colour all the spaces and boxes.

72 - 37 = 35	66 - 29 = 37	82 - 45 = 37	94 - 57 = 37	54 - 17 = 37	63 - 27 = 36	75 - 38 = 37	56 - 19 = 37
90 - 55 = 35	74 - 37 = 37	82 - 48 = 34	84 - 47 = 37	64 - 28 = 36	74 - 38 = 36	93 - 57 = 36	66 - 29 = 37
52 - 17 = 35	93 - 56 = 37	52 - 15 = 37	74 - 37 = 37	95 - 58 = 37	83 - 47 = 36	55 - 18 = 37	63 - 26 = 37
62 - 27 = 35	95 - 58 = 37	73 - 38 = 34	54 - 17 = 37	76 - 39 = 37	94 - 58 = 36	53 - 16 = 37	86 - 49 = 37
71 - 36 = 35	50 - 13 = 37	62 - 28 = 34	83 - 46 = 37	64 - 27 = 37	70 - 34 = 36	84 - 47 = 37	65 - 28 = 37

Copyright © 1999 Brighter Vision Education Ltd 19 Maths, KS2

Page 19

Number Books

Skill: 2-digit subtraction, regrouping

Name ______________________

Colour all the spaces and boxes.

16 — Red
17 — Orange
18 — Yellow

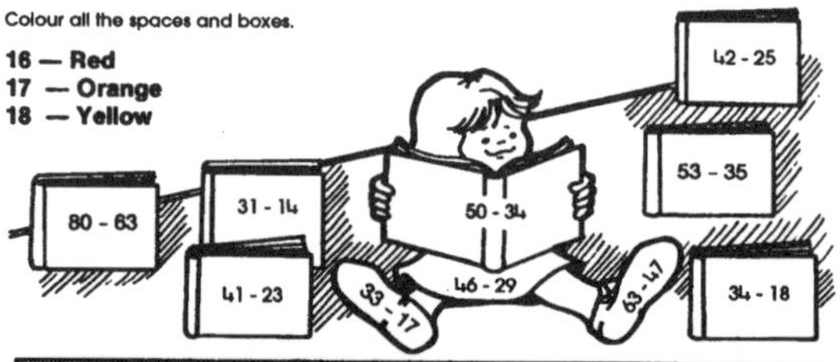

86 - 70 = 16	45 - 29 = 16	70 - 54 = 16	65 - 49 = 16	32 - 14 = 18	94 - 76 = 18	54 - 36 = 18	84 - 66 = 18
91 - 75 = 16	42 - 24 = 18	71 - 53 = 18	57 - 39 = 18	72 - 54 = 18	91 - 73 = 18	35 - 17 = 18	92 - 74 = 18
51 - 35 = 16	42 - 24 = 18	82 - 66 = 16	55 - 39 = 16	93 - 75 = 18	60 - 43 = 17	71 - 54 = 17	95 - 78 = 17
83 - 67 = 16	45 - 27 = 18	54 - 36 = 18	95 - 79 = 16	44 - 26 = 18	62 - 45 = 17	77 - 59 = 18	90 - 73 = 17
61 - 45 = 16	83 - 67 = 16	41 - 25 = 16	80 - 64 = 16	93 - 75 = 18	74 - 57 = 17	40 - 23 = 17	75 - 58 = 17

Copyright © 1999 Brighter Vision Education Ltd 20 Maths, KS2

Page 20

Answer Key

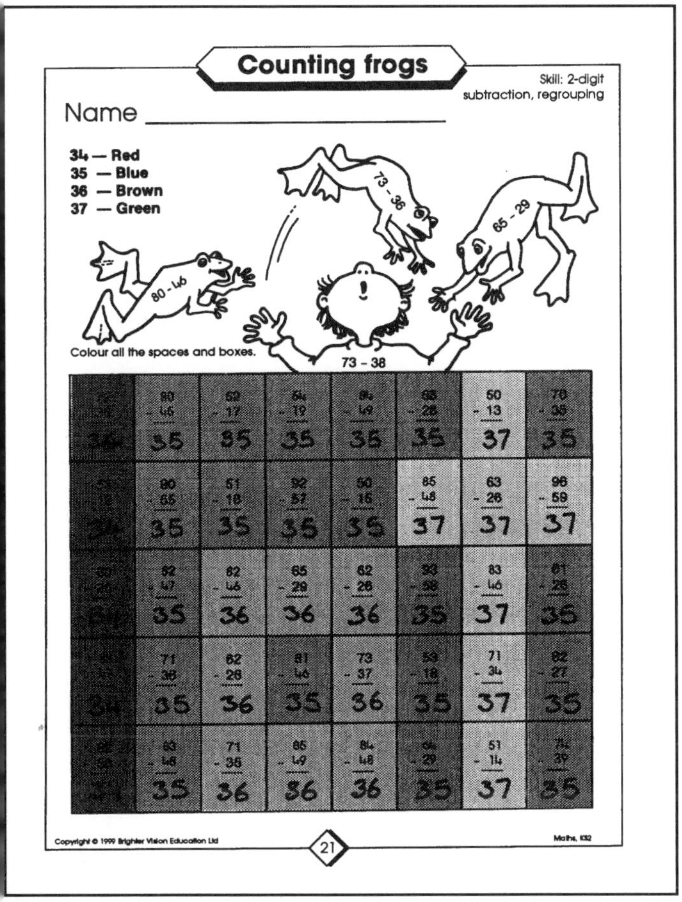

Counting frogs

Skill: 2-digit subtraction, regrouping

Name ____________________

34 — Red
35 — Blue
36 — Brown
37 — Green

73 - 36
65 - 29
80 - 46
73 - 38

Colour all the spaces and boxes.

[illegible] 34	80 − 46 = 35	52 − 17 = 35	54 − 19 = 35	84 − 49 = 35	63 − 28 = 35	50 − 13 = 37	70 − 35 = 35
[illegible] 34	90 − 55 = 35	51 − 16 = 35	92 − 57 = 35	50 − 15 = 35	85 − 48 = 37	63 − 26 = 37	96 − 59 = 37
[illegible] 34	82 − 47 = 35	82 − 46 = 36	65 − 29 = 36	62 − 26 = 36	93 − 58 = 35	83 − 46 = 37	61 − 26 = 35
[illegible] 34	71 − 36 = 35	62 − 26 = 36	81 − 46 = 35	73 − 37 = 36	53 − 18 = 35	71 − 34 = 37	62 − 27 = 35
[illegible] 34	83 − 48 = 35	71 − 35 = 36	85 − 49 = 36	84 − 48 = 36	64 − 29 = 35	51 − 14 = 37	74 − 39 = 35

Page 21

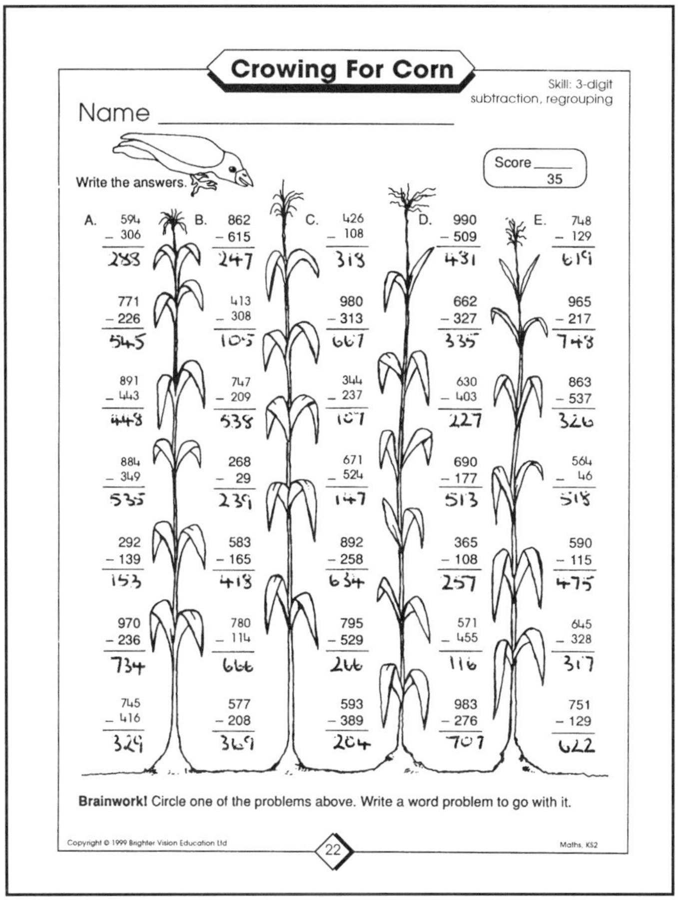

Crowing For Corn

Skill: 3-digit subtraction, regrouping

Name ____________________

Score ___ / 35

Write the answers.

A.	B.	C.	D.	E.
594 − 306 = 288	862 − 615 = 247	426 − 108 = 318	990 − 509 = 481	748 − 129 = 619
771 − 226 = 545	413 − 308 = 105	980 − 313 = 667	662 − 327 = 335	965 − 217 = 748
891 − 443 = 448	747 − 209 = 538	344 − 237 = 107	630 − 403 = 227	863 − 537 = 326
884 − 349 = 535	268 − 29 = 239	671 − 524 = 147	690 − 177 = 513	564 − 46 = 518
292 − 139 = 153	583 − 165 = 418	892 − 258 = 634	365 − 108 = 257	590 − 115 = 475
970 − 236 = 734	780 − 114 = 666	795 − 529 = 266	571 − 455 = 116	645 − 328 = 317
745 − 416 = 329	577 − 208 = 369	593 − 389 = 204	983 − 276 = 707	751 − 129 = 622

Brainwork! Circle one of the problems above. Write a word problem to go with it.

Page 22

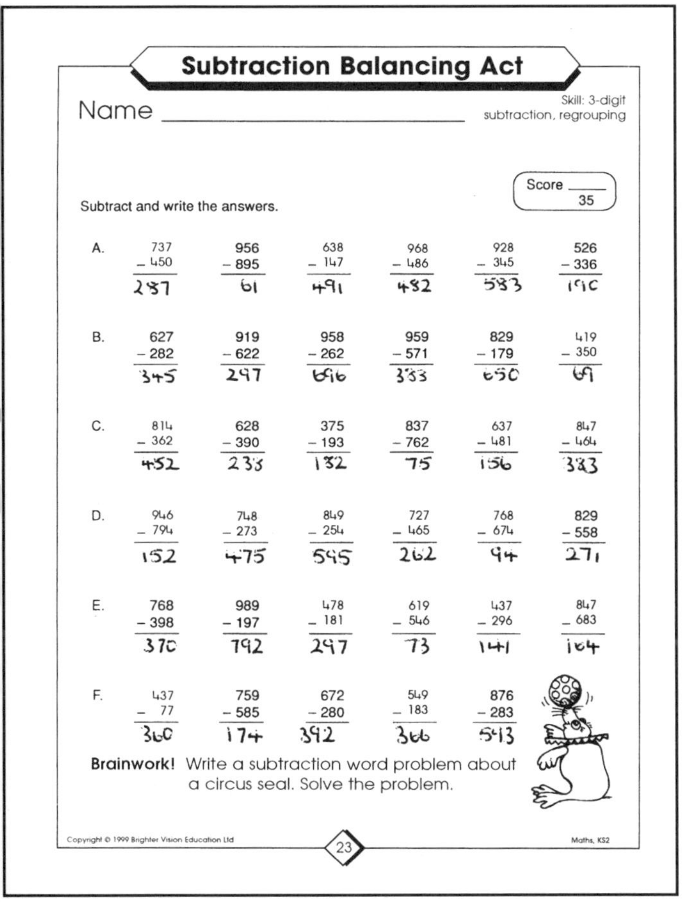

Subtraction Balancing Act

Name ____________________

Skill: 3-digit subtraction, regrouping

Score ___ / 35

Subtract and write the answers.

A.	737 − 450 = 287	956 − 895 = 61	638 − 147 = 491	968 − 486 = 482	928 − 345 = 583	526 − 336 = 190
B.	627 − 282 = 345	919 − 622 = 297	958 − 262 = 696	959 − 571 = 388	829 − 179 = 650	419 − 350 = 69
C.	814 − 362 = 452	628 − 390 = 238	375 − 193 = 182	837 − 762 = 75	637 − 481 = 156	847 − 464 = 383
D.	946 − 794 = 152	748 − 273 = 475	849 − 254 = 595	727 − 465 = 262	768 − 674 = 94	829 − 558 = 271
E.	768 − 398 = 370	989 − 197 = 792	478 − 181 = 297	619 − 546 = 73	437 − 296 = 141	847 − 683 = 164
F.	437 − 77 = 360	759 − 585 = 174	672 − 280 = 392	549 − 183 = 366	876 − 283 = 593	

Brainwork! Write a subtraction word problem about a circus seal. Solve the problem.

Page 23

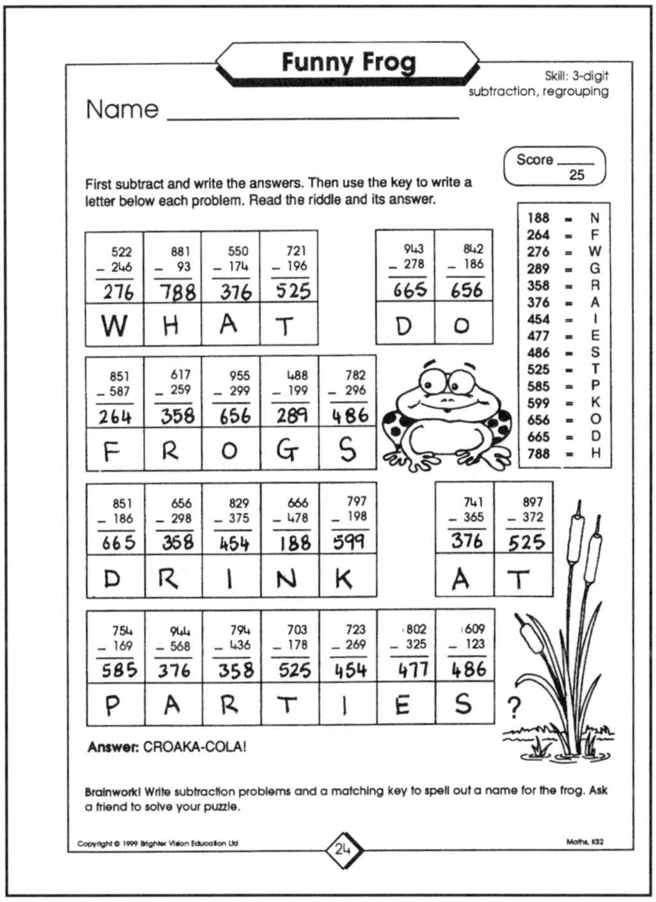

Funny Frog

Skill: 3-digit subtraction, regrouping

Name ____________________

Score ___ / 25

First subtract and write the answers. Then use the key to write a letter below each problem. Read the riddle and its answer.

522 − 246 = 276	881 − 93 = 788	550 − 174 = 376	721 − 196 = 525		943 − 278 = 665	842 − 186 = 656
W	H	A	T		D	O
851 − 587 = 264	617 − 259 = 358	955 − 299 = 656	488 − 199 = 289	782 − 296 = 486		
F	R	O	G	S		
851 − 186 = 665	656 − 298 = 358	829 − 375 = 454	666 − 478 = 188	797 − 198 = 599	741 − 365 = 376	897 − 372 = 525
D	R	I	N	K	A	T
754 − 169 = 585	944 − 568 = 376	794 − 436 = 358	703 − 178 = 525	723 − 269 = 454	802 − 325 = 477	609 − 123 = 486
P	A	R	T	I	E	S ?

188	N
264	F
276	W
289	G
358	R
376	A
454	I
477	E
486	S
525	T
585	P
599	K
656	O
665	D
788	H

Answer: CROAKA-COLA!

Brainwork! Write subtraction problems and a matching key to spell out a name for the frog. Ask a friend to solve your puzzle.

Page 24

Answer Key

Cat and Mouse Maze

Name ______________________

Skill: 3-digit subtraction, with/without regrouping

Score 40

Help mouse run to a hole before Cat wakes up. Subtract and write the answers. Then begin at the START and colour all the boxes with answers that are even numbers.

START	A. 289 − 143 = 146	856 − 198 = 658	707 − 158 = 549	857 − 812 = 45	709 − 102 = 607
B. 645 − 272 = 373	932 − 285 = 647	302 − 146 = 156	682 − 381 = 301	529 − 120 = 409	685 − 192 = 493
C. 749 − 334 = 415	456 − 109 = 347	582 − 498 = 84	838 − 770 = 68	511 − 165 = 346	999 − 283 = 716
D. 566 − 233 = 333	889 − 266 = 623	631 − 328 = 303	458 − 291 = 167	953 − 776 = 177	804 − 128 = 676
E. 880 − 449 = 431	787 − 184 = 603	628 − 493 = 135	489 − 72 = 417	809 − 139 = 670	458 − 228 = 230
F. 250 − 89 = 161	179 − 126 = 53	581 − 126 = 455	818 − 191 = 627	832 − 678 = 154	501 − 178 = 323
G. 493 − 256 = 237	357 − 108 = 249	701 − 204 = 497	510 − 99 = 411	849 − 101 = 748	

Brainwork! Write a word problem to match one of the problems above.

Page 25

Zeros Are Important

Name ______________________

Skill: 2 to 5-digit subtraction

A. Subtract. Add to check your answers.

1. 207 − 143 = 64; 64 + 143 = 207
2. 100 − 64 = 36; 36 + 64 = 100
3. 602 − 314 = 288; 288 + 314 = 602
4. 5,007 − 2,106 = 2,901; 2,901 + 2,106 = 5,007
5. 4,109 − 1,174 = 2,935; 2,935 + 1,174 = 4,109
6. 3,000 − 2,674 = 326; 326 + 2,674 = 3,000
7. 9,008 − 3,962 = 5,046; 5,046 + 3,962 = 9,008
8. 12,003 − 10,666 = 1,337; 1,337 + 10,666 = 12,003
9. 70,405 − 21,510 = 48,895; 48,895 + 21,510 = 70,405 (largest)

B. Write the problems below in column form and subtract. Write the answers in correct order from smallest to largest.

1. 560 − 392 = 168
2. 4,300 − 571 = 3729
3. 5,000 − 297 = 4703
4. 640 − 399 = 241
5. 7,040 − 2,607 = 4433
6. 1,007 − 352 = 655

smallest

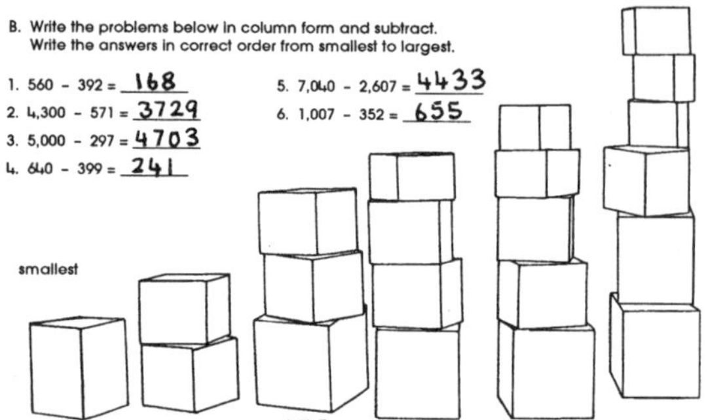

1. 168 2. 241 3. 655 4. 3729 5. 4433 6. 4703

Page 26

Working with Numbers

Name ______________________

Skill: 4-Digit subtraction

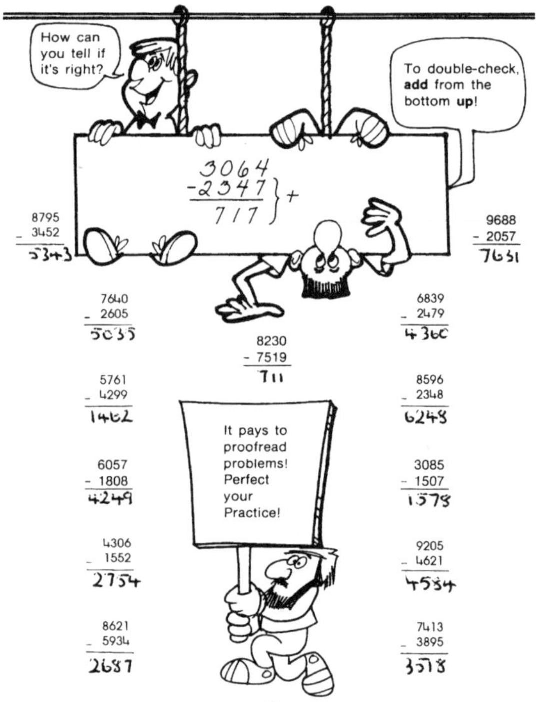

- 8795 − 3452 = 5343
- 9688 − 2057 = 7631
- 7640 − 2605 = 5035
- 6839 − 2479 = 4360
- 8230 − 7519 = 711
- 5761 − 4299 = 1462
- 8596 − 2348 = 6248
- 6057 − 1808 = 4249
- 3085 − 1507 = 1578
- 4306 − 1552 = 2754
- 9205 − 4621 = 4584
- 8621 − 5934 = 2687
- 7413 − 3895 = 3518

Page 27

Keep on track

Name ______________________

Skill: Addition and subtraction: 3 and 4-digit numbers

Begin the race and continue on the track. Add or subtract the amounts shown in the key.

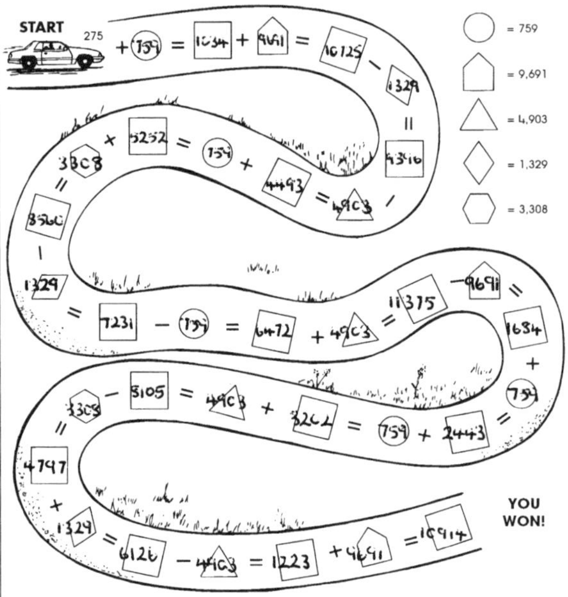

- circle = 759
- pentagon = 9,691
- triangle = 4,903
- diamond = 1,329
- hexagon = 3,308

Page 28

Answer Key

Talk With the Animals

Name ____________________

Skill: Adding and subtracting 3, 4 and 5-digit numbers

Add or subtract. Use your answers to write and solve a riddle.

O. 5,038 + 2,847 = 7885

W. 6,034 − 2,993 = 3041

N. 7,645 + 8,397 = 16042

C. 57,634 + 18,906 = 76540

D. 9,634 − 5,798 = 3836

E. 3,497 + 867 = 4364

K. 4,263 − 1,896 = 2367

H. 9,156 + 8,375 = 17531

P. 54,375 − 36,693 = 17682

L. 3,073 − 897 = 2176

U. 5,372 − 439 = 4933

A. 23,842 − 1,632 = 22210

S. 32,693 + 41,221 = 73914

I. 14,734 − 2,961 = 11773

F. 1,646 + 1,826 = 3472 G. 9,874 − 8,887 = 987 T. 4,419 + 2,987 = 7406

W H A T (3,041 17,531 22,210 7,406) D O E S (3,836 7,885 4,364 73,914) A (22,210)

C H I C K E N (76,540 17,531 11,773 76,540 2,367 4,364 16,042) S P E A K? (73,914 17,682 4,364 22,210 2,367)

F O W L (3,472 7,885 3,041 2,176) L A N G U A G E (2,176 22,210 16,042 987 4,993 22,210 987 4,364)

 29 Maths, KS2

Page 29

Tracking Down Facts?

Name ____________________

Skill: Multiplication facts, 0-9 as factors

Write the missing factor or product.

A.
6 x 5 = 30
8 x 4 = 32
7 x 3 = 21
9 x 9 = 81
0 x 4 = 0
9 x 3 = 27
6 x 2 = 12
4 x 4 = 16
8 x 5 = 40
3 x 3 = 9

B.
3 x 8 = 24
5 x 4 = 20
0 x 3 = 0
8 x 1 = 8
2 x 7 = 14
5 x 5 = 25
6 x 9 = 54
6 x 4 = 24
7 x 6 = 42
3 x 4 = 12

C.
2 x 5 = 10
7 x 7 = 49
3 x 5 = 15
8 x 2 = 16
6 x 6 = 36
9 x 7 = 63
5 x 9 = 45
2 x 2 = 4
1 x 0 = 0
3 x 6 = 18

D.
2 x 4 = 8
1 x 7 = 7
6 x 8 = 48
8 x 5 = 40
3 x 1 = 3
5 x 7 = 35
8 x 9 = 72
3 x 2 = 6
7 x 4 = 28
8 x 8 = 64

E.
9 x 4 = 36
5 x 6 = 30
1 x 7 = 7
1 x 5 = 5
0 x 6 = 0
1 x 1 = 1
4 x 9 = 36
2 x 9 = 18
0 x 2 = 0
7 x 8 = 56

Score ___ / 50

Brainwork! Write four multiplication problems that have 7 as a missing factor.

 30 Maths, KS2

Page 30

Beat the Clock!

Name ____________________

Skill: Multiplication facts, 0-10 as factors

A. Complete this chart by multiplying.

Example:

X	1	2
1	1	2
2	2	4

Can you finish it in five minutes or less?

Score ___ / 100

X	1	2	3	4	5	6	7	8	9	10
1	1	2	3	4	5	6	7	8	9	10
2	2	4	6	8	10	12	14	16	18	20
3	3	6	9	12	15	18	21	24	27	30
4	4	8	12	16	20	24	28	32	36	40
5	5	10	15	20	25	30	35	40	45	50
6	6	12	18	24	30	36	42	48	54	60
7	7	14	21	28	35	42	49	56	63	70
8	8	16	24	32	40	48	56	64	72	80
9	9	18	27	36	45	54	63	72	81	90
10	10	20	30	40	50	60	70	80	90	100

X	7	1	5	2	6	9	3	8	0	4
4	28	4	20	8	24	36	12	32	0	16
9	63	9	45	18	54	81	27	72	0	36
6	42	6	30	12	36	54	18	48	0	24
1	7	1	5	2	6	9	3	8	0	4
5	35	5	25	10	30	45	15	40	0	20
8	56	8	40	16	48	72	24	64	0	32
0	0	0	0	0	0	0	0	0	0	0
3	21	3	15	6	18	27	9	24	0	12
7	49	7	35	14	42	63	21	56	0	28
2	14	2	10	4	12	18	6	16	0	8

B. This multiplication chart is a little harder because the numbers are out of order.

Can you finish it in eight minutes or less?

Score ___ / 100

 31 Maths, KS2

Page 31

Multiplying All Around

Name ____________________

Skill: Multiplying 1-9 as factors

Multiply the centre numbers by the numbers in the middle rings.

 32 Maths, KS2

Page 32

Answer Key

Know-It-All Knights

Skill: Multiplying by 5 and 6

Name ____________________

Write each product. Cross off the answer on the matching shield.

A.
4 x 5 = 20
3 x 5 = 15
8 x 5 = 40
7 x 5 = 35
0 x 5 = 0
9 x 5 = 45
5 x 5 = 25
1 x 5 = 5
6 x 5 = 30
2 x 5 = 10

B.
3 x 6 = 18
1 x 6 = 6
6 x 6 = 36
5 x 6 = 30
9 x 6 = 54
0 x 6 = 0
7 x 6 = 42
2 x 6 = 12
8 x 6 = 48
4 x 6 = 24

Solve each problem.

C. 6 x 7 42	D. 5 x 8 40	E. 5 x 3 15	F. 6 x 4 24	G. 5 x 7 35	H. 6 x 5 30
I. 6 x 6 36	J. 6 x 0 0	K. 5 x 5 25	L. 6 x 9 54	M. 5 x 9 45	N. 5 x 1 5
O. 5 x 4 20	P. 6 x 8 48	Q. 5 x 7 35	R. 6 x 2 12		Score 36

Brainwork! If a number is multiplied by 5, the answer will always end in one of two numbers. Write the two numbers.

Page 33

Kangaroo Fun

Skill: Multiplying by 5, 6, 7, 8 and 9

Name ____________________

Multiply and write the answers.

A.
3 x 7 = 21
5 x 9 = 45
0 x 6 = 0
4 x 5 = 20
1 x 8 = 8
9 x 7 = 63
3 x 6 = 18
2 x 8 = 16
8 x 5 = 40
4 x 9 = 36

B.
6 x 8 = 48
8 x 9 = 72
5 x 6 = 30
1 x 5 = 5
4 x 7 = 28
0 x 9 = 0
8 x 6 = 48
3 x 5 = 15
7 x 7 = 49
9 x 8 = 72

C.
5 x 5 = 25
6 x 6 = 36
2 x 7 = 14
0 x 8 = 0
3 x 9 = 18
7 x 5 = 35
1 x 9 = 9
4 x 8 = 32
9 x 6 = 54
6 x 7 = 42

D.
7 x 6 = 42
0 x 5 = 0
9 x 9 = 81
1 x 7 = 7
3 x 8 = 24
7 x 9 = 63
2 x 5 = 10
8 x 7 = 56
5 x 8 = 40
2 x 6 = 12

E.
1 x 6 = 6
7 x 8 = 56
6 x 5 = 30
6 x 9 = 54
5 x 7 = 35
9 x 5 = 45
2 x 9 = 18
4 x 6 = 24
8 x 8 = 64
0 x 7 = 0

Brainwork! Write a word problem about kangaroos that can be solved using a multiplication fact from this page.

Page 34

Skydiving

Skill: Multiplying by 7 and 8

Name ____________________

Write each product. Cross off the answer on the matching parachute.

A.
4 x 7 = 28
7 x 7 = 49
1 x 7 = 7
3 x 7 = 21
5 x 7 = 35
6 x 7 = 42
0 x 7 = 0
2 x 7 = 14
9 x 7 = 63
8 x 7 = 56

B.
8 x 8 = 64
3 x 8 = 24
0 x 8 = 0
7 x 8 = 56
4 x 8 = 32
1 x 8 = 8
6 x 8 = 48
9 x 8 = 72
2 x 8 = 16
5 x 8 = 40

Solve each problem.

C. 8 x 6 48	D. 7 x 1 7	E. 7 x 5 35	F. 8 x 4 32	G. 7 x 7 49	H. 8 x 8 64
I. 8 x 5 40	J. 8 x 0 0	K. 7 x 9 63	L. 8 x 3 24	M. 8 x 9 72	N. 7 x 2 14
O. 7 x 3 21	P. 7 x 8 56	Q. 8 x 2 16	R. 7 x 6 42		Score 36

Brainwork! Write a word problem that can be solved using this fact: 7 x 8 = 56

Page 35

A Bright Bouquet

Skill: Multiplying by 9 and 10

Name ____________________

Write each product. Cross off the answer on the matching flowers.

A.
2 x 9 = 18
9 x 9 = 81
0 x 9 = 0
3 x 9 = 27
4 x 9 = 36
10 x 9 = 90
7 x 9 = 63
1 x 9 = 9
5 x 9 = 45
8 x 9 = 72
6 x 9 = 54

B.
5 x 10 = 50
3 x 10 = 30
10 x 10 = 100
7 x 10 = 70
0 x 10 = 0
2 x 10 = 20
6 x 10 = 60
1 x 10 = 10
8 x 10 = 80
9 x 10 = 90
4 x 10 = 40

Solve each problem.

C. 9 x 9 18	D. 10 x 0 0	E. 9 x 3 27	F. 10 x 4 40	G. 9 x 8 72	H. 10 x 6 60
I. 9 x 6 54	J. 9 x 1 9	K. 10 x 5 50	L. 9 x 7 63	M. 10 x 9 90	N. 10 x 10 100
O. 10 x 3 30	P. 9 x 2 18	Q. 9 x 4 36	R. 10 x 8 80		Score 38

Brainwork! Look at your answers for problems with 9 as a factor. If you add the digits in each answer, what number will you always get? 9

Page 36

Answer Key

Terrific Tens

Skill: Multiplying by multiples of 10

Name ____________________

Multiply.

A. 6 x 1 = 6
6 x 10 = 60

B. 3 x 4 = 12
3 x 40 = 120

C. 5 x 7 = 35
5 x 70 = 350

D. 8 x 2 = 16
8 x 20 = 160

E. 6 x 6 = 36
6 x 60 = 360

F. 9 x 6 = 54
9 x 60 = 540

G. 4 x 7 = 28
40 x 7 = 280

H. 8 x 5 = 40
8 x 50 = 400

I. 9 x 3 = 27
90 x 3 = 270

J. 7 x 3 = 21
7 x 30 = 210

K. 5 x 5 = 25
50 x 5 = 250

L. 7 x 0 = 0
70 x 0 = 0

M. 4 x 8 = 32
4 x 80 = 320

N. 3 x 6 = 18
30 x 6 = 180

O. 8 x 8 = 64
80 x 8 = 640

Solve each problem.

P. 20 x 9 = 180	Q. 20 x 3 = 60	R. 30 x 5 = 150	S. 40 x 4 = 160	T. 50 x 2 = 100	U. 90 x 9 = 810
V. 80 x 9 = 720	W. 70 x 7 = 490	X. 40 x 0 = 0	Y. 10 x 8 = 80		Score ___ / 40

Brainwork! Use these numbers (3, 4, 6, 8, 30, 40, 60, 80) to write four multiplication problems whose answer is 240.

Page 37

Happy Hundreds

Skill: Multiplying by multiples of 100

Name ____________________

Multiply.

A. 4 x 1 = 4
4 x 10 = 40
4 x 100 = 400

B. 7 x 3 = 21
7 x 30 = 210
7 x 300 = 2100

C. 9 x 9 = 81
9 x 90 = 810
9 x 900 = 8100

D. 5 x 6 = 30
50 x 6 = 300
500 x 6 = 3000

E. 8 x 7 = 56
8 x 70 = 560
800 x 7 = 5600

F. 6 x 2 = 12
60 x 2 = 120
6 x 200 = 1200

G. 8 x 8 = 64
80 x 8 = 640
800 x 8 = 6400

H. 4 x 5 = 20
4 x 50 = 200
4 x 500 = 2000

Solve each problem.

I. 800 x 6 = 4800	J. 900 x 4 = 3600	K. 500 x 5 = 2500	L. 300 x 8 = 2400	M. 700 x 2 = 1400	N. 400 x 6 = 2400
O. 200 x 2 = 400	P. 400 x 8 = 3200	Q. 600 x 7 = 4200	R. 900 x 0 = 0	S. 300 x 6 = 1800	T. 400 x 2 = 800
U. 100 x 7 = 700	V. 200 x 5 = 1000	W. 600 x 9 = 5400	X. 300 x 3 = 900		Score ___ / 40

Brainwork! Study the pattern above. Then solve these problems.
7 x 3,000 = 21,000   9,000 x 8 = 72,000   2 x 60,000 = 120,000

Page 38

Fanciful Flight

Skill: Multiplying 2-digit by 1-digit numbers, regrouping

Name ____________________

Solve each problem by multiplying.
Cross off the answer on the butterfly.

Score ___ / 25

67 x 5 = 335	A. 19 x 2 = 38	B. 34 x 8 = 272	C. 63 x 9 = 567	D. 15 x 8 = 120
E. 49 x 5 = 245	F. 53 x 6 = 318	G. 27 x 4 = 108	H. 37 x 3 = 111	I. 28 x 7 = 196
J. 48 x 9 = 432	K. 65 x 3 = 195	L. 17 x 7 = 119	M. 88 x 2 = 176	N. 61 x 6 = 366
O. 86 x 8 = 688	P. 24 x 4 = 96	Q. 55 x 5 = 275	R. 31 x 9 = 279	S. 56 x 7 = 392
		T. 36 x 3 = 108	U. 42 x 6 = 252	V. 93 x 4 = 372
		W. 85 x 2 = 170	X. 39 x 7 = 273	Y. 19 x 8 = 152

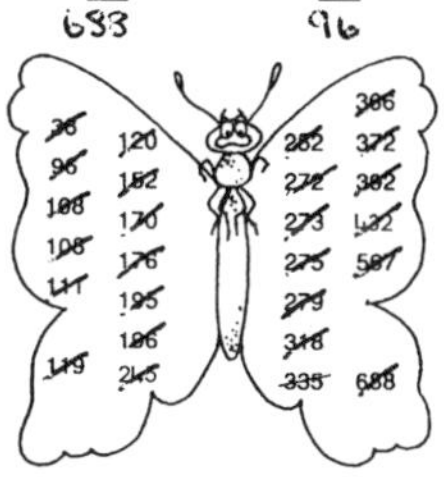

Brainwork! If Dawn saw 13 butterflies and each had 6 spots on its wings, how many butterfly spots did she see?

Page 39

Up, Up and Away

Skill: Multiplying by 2-digit numbers

Name ____________________

Multiply. Put the letters of the answers on the lines below to find out a secret message.

J: 159 x 47 = 1113 + 6360 = 7473

T: 454 x 60 = 0 + 27240 = 27240

G: 719 x 18 = 5752 + 7190 = 12942

O: 295 x 65 = 1475 + 17700 = 19175

R: 607 x 45 = 3035 + 24280 = 27315

!: 106 x 85 = 530 + 8480 = 9010

E: 599 x 12 = 1198 + 5990 = 7188

B: 333 x 65 = 1665 + 19980 = 21645

A: 682 x 23 = 2046 + 13640 = 15686

G	R	E	A	T		J	O	B	!
12,942	27,315	7,188	15,686	27,240		7,473	19,175	21,645	9,010

Page 40

Answer Key

Get in Shape

Skill: Multiplying by 2-digit numbers

Name ____________________

Multiply.

A.

79 × 21 = 1659	34 × 67 = 2278	57 × 60 = 3420	29 × 16 = 464

B.

603 × 19 = 11457	101 × 38 = 3838	900 × 35 = 31500	816 × 68 = 55488

C.

144 × 30 = 4320	175 × 14 = 2450	809 × 24 = 19416	96 × 25 = 2400

D.

961 × 40 = 38440	506 × 12 = 6072	56 × 22 = 1232	63 × 18 = 1134

 41 Maths, KS2

Page 41

Digit Disease

Skill: Multiplication: 3 Digits x 2 Digits

Name ____________________

Multiply. Then add the products.

674 × 27: 4718 + 13480 = 18198	450 × 65: 2250 + 27000 = 29250	917 × 25: 4585 + 18340 = 22925	542 × 73: 1626 + 37940 = 39566	406 × 26: 2436 + 8120 = 10556
853 × 74: 3412 + 59710 = 63122	346 × 54: 1384 + 17300 = 18684	902 × 48: 7216 + 36080 = 43296	300 × 46: 1800 + 12000 = 13800	761 × 25: 3805 + 15220 = 19025
674 × 27: 4718 + 13480 = 18198	808 × 34: 3232 + 24240 = 27472	432 × 59: 3888 + 21600 = 25488	735 × 74: 2940 + 51450 = 54390	207 × 98: 1656 + 18630 = 20286
327 × 58: 2616 + 16350 = 18966	772 × 48: 6176 + 30880 = 37056	307 × 59: 2763 + 15350 = 18113	912 × 79: 8208 + 63840 = 72048	686 × 68: 5488 + 41160 = 46648

 42 Maths, KS2

Page 42

Review

Skill: Review

Name ____________________

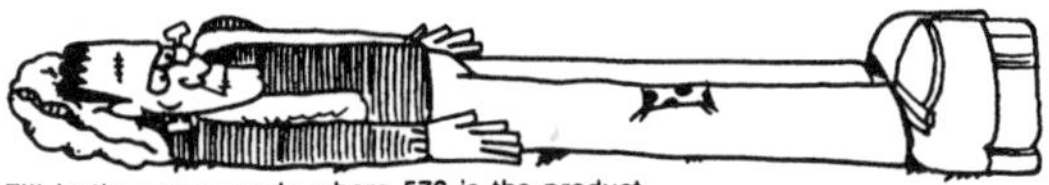

Fill in the spaces only where 576 is the product.

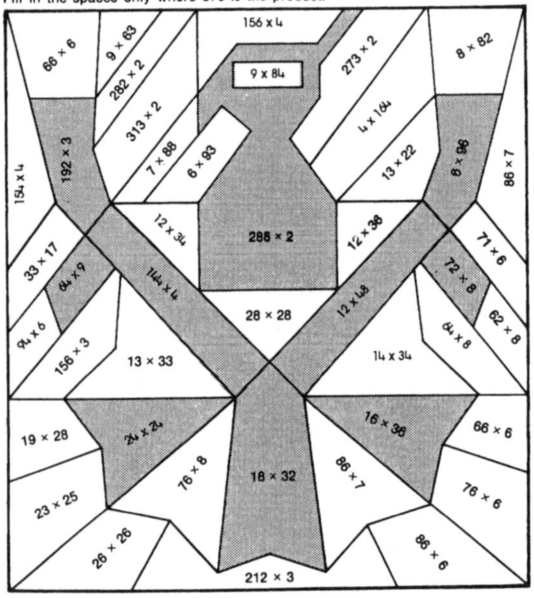

 43 Maths, KS2

Page 43

Review

Skill: Review

Name ____________________

When is a bright idea like a clock?

When i t s t r i k e s o n e
(1 2 3 4 5 6 7 8 9 10 11 12)

Directions: Solve each division problem. Find the quotient and matching letter in the code box below to answer the riddle.

1. 4) 72 = 18	2. 3) 1458 = 486	3. 7) 161 = 23	4. 6) 2916 = 486
5. 2) 94 = 47	6. 9) 162 = 18	7. 5) 385 = 77	8. 4) 2756 = 689
9. 5) 115 = 23	10. 8) 464 = 58	11. 6) 150 = 25	12. 9) 6201 = 689

18	23	25	47	58	77	486	689
i	s	n	r	o	k	t	e

 44 Maths, KS2

Page 44

Answer Key

Get Your Facts Straight

Name ____________________ Skill: Special products

Complete each equation with a different factor pair. (Hint: Use multiplication facts to help you.)

A. 800
10 x 80
20 x 40
1 x 800

B. 1,000
10 x 100
20 x 50
1 x 1000

C. 1,500
30 x 50
15 x 100
60 x 25

D. 1,200
30 x 40
20 x 60
10 x 120
80 x 15

E. 16,000
80 x 200
40 x 400
20 x 800
10 x 1600

F. 20,000
10 x 2000
20 x 1000
40 x 500
80 x 250

G. 4,000
10 x 400
20 x 200
40 x 100
8 x 500

H. 240,000
100 x 2400
200 x 1200
300 x 800
400 x 600

Shade in the factors that you could NOT use. Then turn your paper so that the right side of the page is at the top. You will see what all of these numbers have in common.

~~10~~	~~40~~	70	90	70,000	700	~~30~~	~~200~~	90,000
~~30~~	300	700	~~20~~	700	~~60~~	70	~~40~~	9,000
~~80~~	500	900	~~60~~	9,000	~~50~~	~~400~~	90	9
7	90	7,000	900	90,000	~~100~~	~~10~~	~~20~~	7,000

Page 45

Moving Along

Skill: Dividing 1-9

Name ____________________

Divide each problem. Write the quotient as the divisor for the next problem. Write each final answer in a circle.

1. 5)25 = 5 → 5)40 = 8 → 8)56 = 7 → 7)63 = 9 → 9)54 = 6 (6)
2. 9)18 = 2 → 2)18 = 9 → 9)81 = 9 → 9)72 = 8 → 8)64 = 8 (8)
3. 4)36 = 9 → 9)27 = 3 → 3)21 = 7 → 7)63 = 9 → 9)36 = 4 (4)
4. 5)40 = 8 → 8)16 = 2 → 2)16 = 8 → 8)24 = 3 → 3)18 = 6 (6)
5. 6)30 = 5 → 5)45 = 9 → 9)45 = 5 → 5)10 = 2 → 2)8 = 4 (4)
6. 7)35 = 5 → 5)20 = 4 → 4)32 = 8 → 8)24 = 3 → 3)21 = 7 (7)
7. 2)4 = 2 → 2)10 = 5 → 5)15 = 3 → 3)18 = 6 → 6)30 = 5 (5)
8. 5)35 = 7 → 7)14 = 2 → 2)16 = 8 → 8)64 = 8 → 8)32 = 4 (4)

Shade in the answers that are correct.

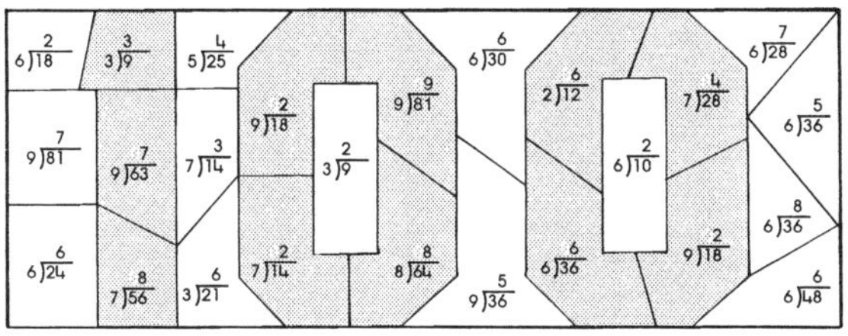

Page 46

A Riddle

Name ____________________ Skill: Division, divisors of 1, 7

Riddle: Why are elephants so wrinkled?

HAVE YOU EVER TRIED TO IRON ONE?

H A V E (4 1 0 5) Y O U (12 9 8) E V E R (5 0 5 6) T R I E D (3 6 10 5 7) T O (3 9) I R O N (10 6 9 2) O N E (9 2 5)?

A 7)7 = 1	D 7)49 = 7	E 7)35 = 5	H 7)28 = 4
I 1)10 = 10	N 7)14 = 2	O 7)63 = 9	R 7)42 = 6
T 7)21 = 3	U 7)56 = 8	V 7)0 = 0	Y 1)12 = 12

Page 47

A Riddle

Name ____________________ Skill: Division, divisors of 1, 6, 7

How do you send a letter to a fish?

DROP THE FISH A LINE.

D R O P (9 10 6 12) T H E (11 3 8) F I S H (5 2 3) A (7) L I N E (4 2 1 8).

A 6)42 = 7	D 6)54 = 9	E 7)56 = 8	F 7)35 = 5
H 6)18 = 3	I 7)14 = 2	L 7)28 = 4	N 6)6 = 1
O 7)42 = 6	P 6)72 = 12	R 1)10 = 10	T 7)77 = 11

Page 48

Answer Key

Cactus Fun!

Name ____________________

Skill: Division, divisors of 5, 6, 7

DAFFYNITION: A Cactus

A GIANT PINCUSHION

A = 1; G I A N T = 7 5 1 2 0; P I N C U S H I O N = 10 5 2 4 3 8 6 5 9 2

A: 5 ⟌ 5 → 1	C: 6 ⟌ 24 → 4	G: 7 ⟌ 49 → 7	H: 6 ⟌ 36 → 6
I: 6 ⟌ 30 → 5	N: 5 ⟌ 10 → 2	O: 7 ⟌ 63 → 9	P: 5 ⟌ 50 → 10
S: 7 ⟌ 56 → 8	T: 6 ⟌ 0 → 0	U: 5 ⟌ 15 → 3	W: 5 ⟌ 55 → 11

Page 49

Fruit Fun!

Name ____________________

Skill: Division, divisors of 1, 7, 8

Daffynition:

RAISIN: A WORRIED GRAPE

R A I S I N = 9 2 4 10 4 5; A = 2; W O R R I E D = 0 3 9 9 4 6 8; G R A P E = 1 9 2 7 6

A: 8 ⟌ 16 → 2	D: 8 ⟌ 64 → 8	E: 8 ⟌ 48 → 6	G: 7 ⟌ 7 → 1
I: 8 ⟌ 32 → 4	N: 7 ⟌ 35 → 5	O: 7 ⟌ 21 → 3	P: 7 ⟌ 49 → 7
R: 8 ⟌ 72 → 9	S: 1 ⟌ 10 → 10	W: 8 ⟌ 0 → 0	Y: 8 ⟌ 88 → 11

Page 50

A Tongue Twister

Name ____________________

Skill: Division, divisors of 8, 9

BLOWING DOUBLE BUBBLE GUM DOUBLES BUBBLES.

B L O W I N G = 3 8 4 12 10 0 7; D O U B L E = 6 4 5 3 8 2

B U B B L E = 3 5 3 3 8 2; G U M = 7 5 9; D O U B L E S = 6 4 5 3 8 2 1

B U B B L E S = 3 5 3 3 8 2 1

B: 8 ⟌ 24 → 3	D: 9 ⟌ 54 → 6	E: 8 ⟌ 16 → 2	G: 9 ⟌ 63 → 7
I: 1 ⟌ 10 → 10	L: 9 ⟌ 72 → 8	M: 9 ⟌ 81 → 9	N: 8 ⟌ 0 → 0
O: 9 ⟌ 36 → 4	S: 8 ⟌ 8 → 1	U: 9 ⟌ 45 → 5	W: 1 ⟌ 12 → 12

Page 51

Apple Division

Name ____________________

Skill: Division, basic facts with remainders

Write each quotient and remainder.
r. : remainder

How can you divide 19 apples equally among 9 boys?

5 ⟌ 12 → 2 r.2	3 ⟌ 10 → 3 r.1	6 ⟌ 14 → 2 r.2	
2 ⟌ 17 → 8 r.1	4 ⟌ 38 → 9 r.2	9 ⟌ 75 → 8 r.3	8 ⟌ 75 → 9 r.3
4 ⟌ 33 → 8 r.1	2 ⟌ 9 → 4 r.1	8 ⟌ 13 → 1 r.5	6 ⟌ 50 → 8 r.2
3 ⟌ 23 → 7 r.2	5 ⟌ 41 → 8 r.1	7 ⟌ 37 → 5 r.2	9 ⟌ 89 → 9 r.8
2 ⟌ 11 → 5 r.1	4 ⟌ 10 → 2 r.2	9 ⟌ 30 → 3 r.3	8 ⟌ 30 → 3 r.6
4 ⟌ 25 → 6 r.1	2 ⟌ 17 → 8 r.1	6 ⟌ 11 → 1 r.5	7 ⟌ 19 → 2 r.5
5 ⟌ 33 → 6 r.3	3 ⟌ 20 → 6 r.2	7 ⟌ 57 → 8 r.1	6 ⟌ 55 → 9 r.1
3 ⟌ 28 → 9 r.1	5 ⟌ 9 → 1 r.4	8 ⟌ 58 → 7 r.2	8 ⟌ 66 → 8 r.2
	4 ⟌ 29 → 7 r.1	7 ⟌ 50 → 7 r.1	7 ⟌ 48 → 6 r.6
		6 ⟌ 39 → 6 r.3	9 ⟌ 46 → 5 r.1
		9 ⟌ 55 → 6 r.1	6 ⟌ 33 → 5 r.3

Make applesauce, of course!

Page 52

Answer Key

A-Mazing Division

Skill: 1- and 2-digit quotients with and without remainders

Name ______________________

Divide. Check by multiplying.

1. 8) 480 = 60 — 60 × 8
2. 9) 369 = 41 — 41 × 9
3. 5) 250 = 50 — 50 × 5
4. 7) 560 = 80 — 80 × 7
5. 6) 240 = 40 — 40 × 6
6. 4) 364 = 91 — 91 × 4

Divide. Watch out for remainders.

7. 9) 60 = 6R6
8. 8) 47 = 5R7
9. 8) 75 = 9R3
10. 4) 31 = 7R3
11. 3) 23 = 7R2
12. 8) 47 = 5R7

Follow your answers through the maze.

Start

60	41	50	80	30	70	91	13	14
40	4R6	5R1	40	91	6R6	8R2	9R1	3R2
70	18	24	6R1	4R2	5R7	7R4	8R2	9R3
5R5	7R3	6R5	5R2	9R1	9R3	7R3	7R2	5R7

You did it!

Page 53

Banana Boat

Skill: Dividing 3-digit numbers

Name ______________________

Divide and write the quotients in the puzzle. Hint: R for remainder will take up its own space.

1	3	1	R	3			5	5	R	2		
	1			7	2	R	3			7		
	R			R						R		6
	2	1		2	8	R	4		8	1	R	3
		0					3					R
	4	1	3	R	1		R				3	7
		R			0		7	9	R	1		
		1			8							

ACROSS

1. 6) 789 = 131R3
4. 6) 332 = 55R2
6. 4) 291 = 72R3
8. 9) 189 = 21
10. 7) 200 = 28R4
12. 8) 651 = 81R3
13. 2) 827 = 413R1
15. 6) 222 = 37
16. 5) 396 = 79R1

DOWN

2. 6) 188 = 31R2
3. 8) 298 = 37R2
4. 4) 212 = 53
5. 9) 244 = 27R1
7. 8) 511 = 63R7
9. 7) 708 = 101R1
11. 9) 394 = 43R7
14. 4) 432 = 108

Page 54

Zero In

Skill: Zeros in quotients

Name ______________________

Divide. Watch out for the zeros.

1. 3) 914 = 304 R2
2. 7) 765 = 109 R2
3. 8) 6472 = 809
4. 6) 609 = 101 R3
5. 5) 800 = 160
6. 9) 975 = 108 R3

Write the quotients above in order from smallest to largest.

1. 101R3 2. 108R3 3. 109R2 4. 160 5. 304R2 6. 809

Write the missing digits in each problem.

7. 5) 250 = 50 R2; 25; 2
8. 6) 498 = 830; 48; 18; 18; 0
9. 4) 203 = 50 R3; 20; 3
10. 9) 8181 = 909; 81; 81; 81; 0
11. 3) 261 = 87; 24; 21; 21; 0
12. 5) 2509 = 501 R4; 25; 09; 5; 4
13. 8) 656 = 82; 64; 16; 16; 0
14. 7) 1435 = 205; 14; 35; 35; 0

Page 55

Divide It Up

Skill: Dividing by 2-digit numbers

Name ______________________

Divide. Write the letter of each problem above its answer below.

I. 34) 2584 = 76
I. 42) 8526 = 203
O. 63) 6237 = 99
D. 55) 3575 = 65
D. 89) 6319 = 71
Y. 90) 1800 = 20
T. 31) 6231 = 201
U. 18) 882 = 49

Y	O	U		D	I	D		I	T	!
20	99	49		65	203	71		76	201	

Find the total test scores below. Then find the averages.

Students	Test Scores					Total	Average
Sue Ann	18	20	17	19	16	90	18
James	15	14	17	16	13	75	15
Tommy	19	19	20	18	19	95	19
Carlos	16	19	18	17	16	86	17.2
Anna	20	20	19	20	19	98	19.6

Who has the highest average? Anna

Who needs to study more? James

Page 56

Answer Key

Doggie Trouble

Skill: Dividing by 2-digit numbers with remainders

Name ____________________

Help the dog get to his bone by connecting the correctly-done division problems to make a path.

23)1972 = 85 R17	32)989 = 30 R29	43)629 = 14 R27	30)6963 = 232 R3	65)6959 = 107 R4
15)1508 = 104 R8	22)687 = 31 R4	19)582 = 31 R12	87)6933 = 78 R6	52)8071 = 155 R11
31)8013 = 255 R15	42)6231 = 14 R15	26)541 = 20 R18	18)819 = 54 R9	26)809 = 31 R3
60)3207 = 52 R27	39)6193 = 158 R31	27)983 = 36 R11	71)8203 = 115 R8	17)989 = 58 R3
		81)1484 = 18 R26	44)1943 = 44 R7	28)1773 = 63 R9

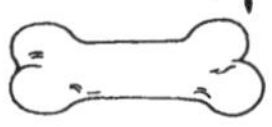

Page 57

Long Division

Skill: Long division: 2-digit dividend

Name ____________________

4 Steps to Success → | Divide, Multiply, Subtract, Pull Down | 1. ÷ 2. × 3. − 4. P.D. | Repeat → | Divide, Multiply, Subtract | 1. ÷ 2. × 3. −

2)72 = 36 6 12 12	8)96 = 12 8 16 16 0	6)84 = 14 6 24 24 0	7)91 = 13 7 21 21 0	3)87 = 29 6 27 27 0
2)74 = 37 6 14 14 0	5)90 = 18 5 40 40 0	7)84 = 12 7 14 14 0	6)96 = 16 6 36 36 0	5)75 = 15 5 25 25 0

Find the quotients and remainders.

5)68 = 13 r.3 5 18 15 3	2)71 = 35 r.1 6 11 10 1	6)79 = 13 r.1 6 19 18 1	7)94 = 13 r.3 7 24 21 3	4)75 = 18 r.3 4 35 32 3
3)74 = 24 r.2 6 14 12 2	6)94 = 15 r.4 6 34 30 4	3)47 = 15 r.2 3 17 15 2	7)99 = 14 r.1 7 29 28 1	6)88 = 14 r.4 6 28 24 4

Page 58

Caterpillar Division

Skill: Long division: 3-digit dividend

Name ____________________

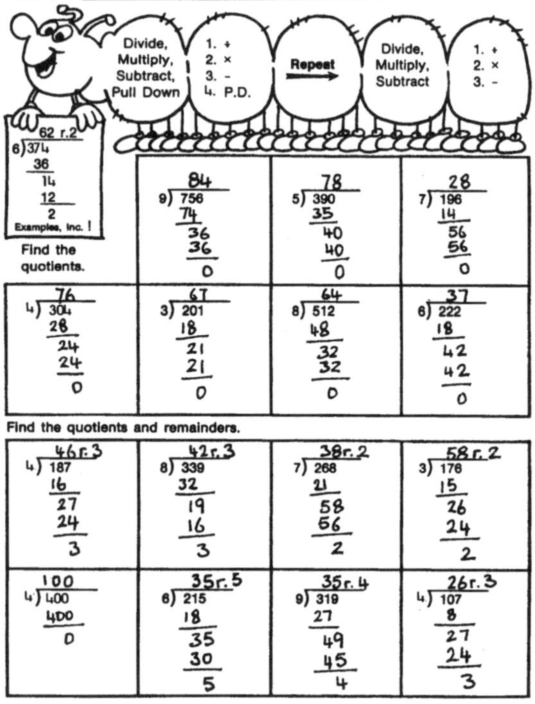

Example: 6)374 = 62 r.2
36
14
12
2

Examples, Inc.!

Find the quotients.

	9)756 = 84 74 36 36 0	5)390 = 78 35 40 40 0	7)196 = 28 14 56 56 0
4)304 = 76 28 24 24 0	3)201 = 67 18 21 21 0	8)512 = 64 48 32 32 0	6)222 = 37 18 42 42 0

Find the quotients and remainders.

4)187 = 46 r.3 16 27 24 3	8)339 = 42 r.3 32 19 16 3	7)268 = 38 r.2 21 58 56 2	3)176 = 58 r.2 15 26 24 2
4)400 = 100 400 0	6)215 = 35 r.5 18 35 30 5	9)319 = 35 r.4 27 49 45 4	4)107 = 26 r.3 8 27 24 3

Page 59

Snake Parts

Skill: Writing fractions

Name ____________________

Write fractions for:

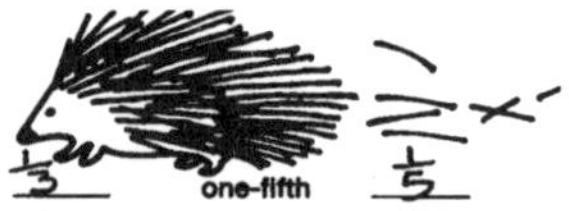

one-half $\frac{1}{2}$ one-third $\frac{1}{3}$ one-fifth $\frac{1}{5}$

one-fourth $\frac{1}{4}$ one-sixth $\frac{1}{6}$ one-tenth $\frac{1}{10}$

one-eighth $\frac{1}{8}$ one-twelfth $\frac{1}{12}$ one-seventh $\frac{1}{7}$

Write fractions for:

one of four parts $\frac{1}{4}$ one of nine parts $\frac{1}{9}$

one of three parts $\frac{1}{3}$ one of six parts $\frac{1}{6}$

one of two parts $\frac{1}{2}$ one of five parts $\frac{1}{5}$

Colour each part as directed.

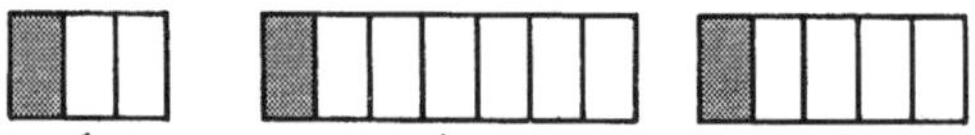

Colour $\frac{1}{3}$ blue. Colour $\frac{1}{7}$ yellow. Colour $\frac{1}{5}$ red.

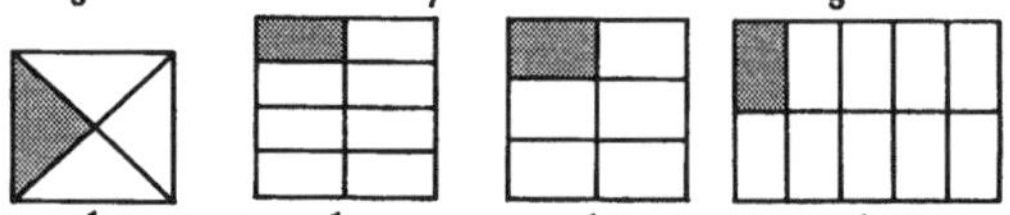

Colour $\frac{1}{4}$ green. Colour $\frac{1}{8}$ orange. Colour $\frac{1}{6}$ brown. Colour $\frac{1}{10}$ black.

Page 60

Answer Key

Pizza Fractions

Skill: Writing fractions

Name ______________________

$\frac{3}{5}$ ← 3 parts are shaded.

There are 5 equal parts. →

Write the fraction for the following **shaded** parts.

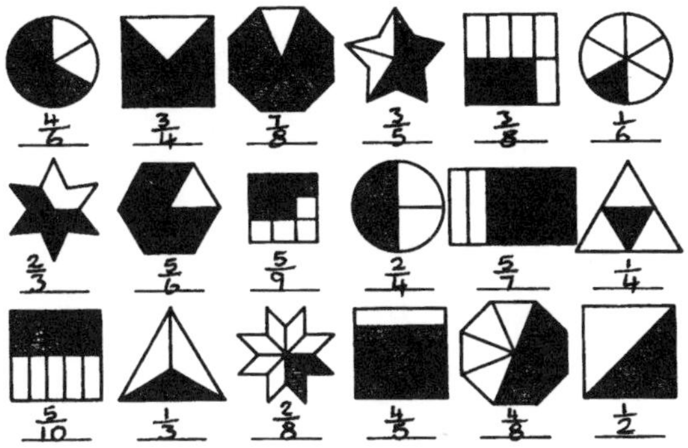

Use These Fractions

$\frac{1}{2}$ $\frac{1}{3}$ $\frac{2}{3}$ $\frac{2}{8}$ $\frac{3}{8}$ $\frac{4}{8}$

$\frac{1}{4}$ $\frac{2}{4}$ $\frac{3}{4}$ $\frac{3}{5}$ $\frac{4}{5}$ $\frac{1}{6}$ $\frac{4}{6}$ $\frac{5}{6}$ $\frac{5}{7}$ $\frac{7}{8}$ $\frac{5}{9}$ $\frac{5}{10}$

 61 Maths, KS2

Page 61

Fraction Pie

Skill: Writing and shading fractions

Name ______________________

Here are two of three equal parts of this circle.

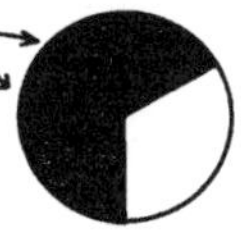

The fraction for "two of three parts" is $\frac{2}{3}$.

Fill in the missing numbers and shade the parts.

"five of six" = $\frac{5}{6}$

"four of five" = $\frac{4}{5}$

"three of eight" = $\frac{3}{8}$

"three of four" = $\frac{3}{4}$

"seven of twelve" = $\frac{7}{12}$

"one of two" = $\frac{1}{2}$

"three of four" = $\frac{3}{4}$

"two of five" = $\frac{2}{5}$

"five of eight" = $\frac{5}{8}$

"nine of ten" = $\frac{9}{10}$

 62 Maths, KS2

Page 62

Snowflake Fun!

Skill: Reducing fractions

Name ______________________

Reduce the fractions below and write them in word form.

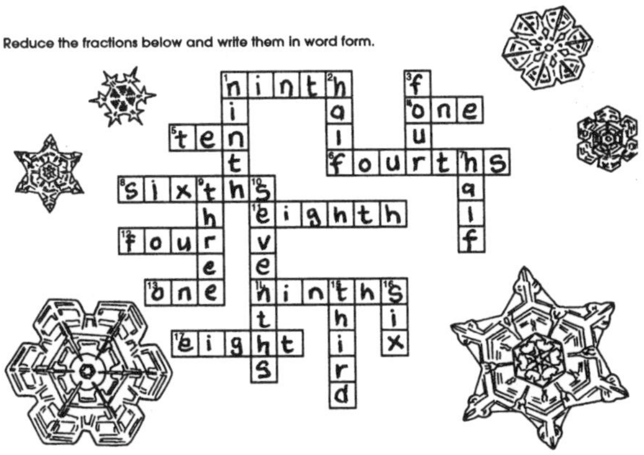

ACROSS

1. $\frac{4}{36}$ = one ninth
4. $\frac{4}{28}$ = one seventh
5. $\frac{30}{33}$ = ten elevenths
6. $\frac{9}{12}$ = three fourths
8. $\frac{15}{18}$ = five sixths
11. $\frac{7}{56}$ = one eight
12. $\frac{16}{36}$ = four ninths
13. $\frac{9}{72}$ = one eighth
14. $\frac{25}{45}$ = five ninths
17. $\frac{24}{33}$ = eight elevenths

DOWN

1. $\frac{3}{27}$ = one ninth
2. $\frac{9}{18}$ = one half
3. $\frac{20}{35}$ = four sevenths
7. $\frac{2}{4}$ = one half
9. $\frac{9}{21}$ = three sevenths
10. $\frac{12}{42}$ = two sevenths
15. $\frac{8}{24}$ = one third
16. $\frac{12}{26}$ = six thirteenths

 63 Maths, KS2

Page 63

Equal Time

Skill: Equivalent fractions

Name ______________________

To find equivalent fractions, the numerator and denominator are multiplied by the same number.

$\frac{1\ (\times 3)}{3\ (\times 3)} = \frac{3}{9}$ $\frac{1\ (\times 6)}{2\ (\times 6)} = \frac{6}{12}$ $\frac{1\ (\times 2)}{4\ (\times 2)} = \frac{2}{8}$

Change each fraction to higher terms.

1. $\frac{1\ (\times 2)}{5\ (\times 2)} = \frac{2}{10}$
2. $\frac{2\ (\times 2)}{5\ (\times 4)} = \frac{2}{10}$
3. $\frac{1\ (\times 2)}{6\ (\times 2)} = \frac{2}{12}$
4. $\frac{2\ (\times 3)}{7\ (\times 6)} = \frac{3}{21}$
5. $\frac{1\ (\times 6)}{2\ (\times 6)} = \frac{6}{12}$
6. $\frac{2\ (\times 4)}{3\ (\times 8)} = \frac{4}{12}$

Multiply in your head. If the equivalents are correct, shade in the areas.

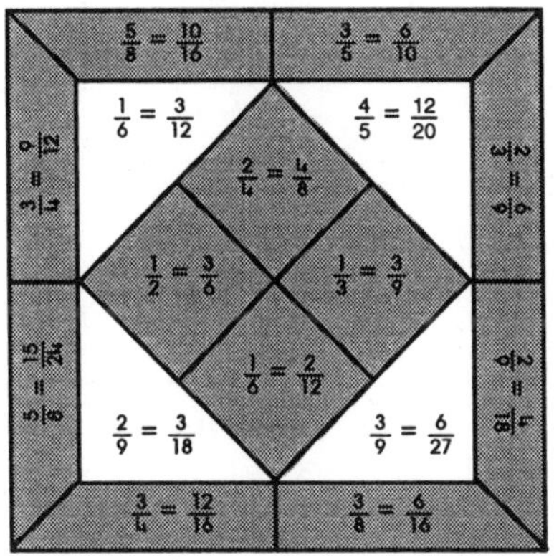

 64 Maths, KS2

Page 64

Answer Key

Bubble Fun

Skill: Improper fractions and mixed numbers

Name ____________________

Change each improper fraction to a mixed number. Or, change each mixed number to an improper fraction.

1. $2\frac{1}{8}$
2. $\frac{5}{4}$
3. $3\frac{1}{4}$
4. $\frac{11}{5}$
5. $5\frac{2}{9}$
6. $\frac{22}{5}$
7. $3\frac{3}{4}$
8. $\frac{32}{9}$
9. $\frac{41}{9}$
10. 5
11. $\frac{41}{8}$
12. 4
13. $\frac{79}{9}$
14. $7\frac{4}{9}$
15. $6\frac{1}{6}$
16. $\frac{38}{5}$
17. $16\frac{3}{5}$
18. $5\frac{4}{7}$

 65 Maths, KS2

Page 65

Let's Compare

Skill: Comparing fractions

Name ____________________

Use >, <, or = to compare the fractions below.

A. $\frac{11}{12} > \frac{8}{9}$ $\frac{3}{4} = \frac{6}{8}$ $\frac{5}{6} > \frac{2}{3}$

B. $\frac{1}{5} < \frac{2}{3}$ $\frac{9}{10} > \frac{3}{4}$ $\frac{2}{5} < \frac{10}{11}$

C. $\frac{2}{5} = \frac{8}{20}$ $\frac{1}{4} < \frac{3}{8}$ $\frac{7}{9} > \frac{3}{4}$

D. $\frac{6}{7} > \frac{2}{5}$ $\frac{4}{7} = \frac{8}{14}$ $\frac{12}{13} > \frac{4}{5}$

 66 Maths, KS2

Page 66

Cloud Crazy

Skill: Adding and subtracting fractions with like denominators

Name ____________________

Add or subtract.

A. $\frac{3}{5} + \frac{1}{5} = \frac{4}{5}$ $\frac{1}{8} + \frac{4}{8} = \frac{5}{8}$ $\frac{1}{4} + \frac{2}{4} = \frac{3}{4}$ $\frac{5}{8} - \frac{3}{8} = \frac{2}{8}$

B. $\frac{7}{8} - \frac{3}{8} = \frac{4}{8}$ $\frac{2}{9} + \frac{5}{9} = \frac{7}{9}$ $\frac{3}{4} - \frac{1}{4} = \frac{2}{4}$ $\frac{1}{12} + \frac{3}{12} = \frac{4}{12}$

C. $\frac{7}{12} - \frac{1}{12} = \frac{6}{12}$ $\frac{3}{8} + \frac{5}{8} = \frac{8}{8}$ $\frac{5}{9} + \frac{1}{9} = \frac{6}{9}$ $\frac{2}{3} - \frac{1}{3} = \frac{1}{3}$

 67 Maths, KS2

Page 66

X Marks the Spot

Skill: Solving proportions

Name ____________________

Solve for x. Shade in the answers in the box below. Your answers will form a design.

A. $\frac{5}{6} = \frac{x}{24}$ x = 20 $\frac{1}{4} = \frac{x}{20}$ x = 5 $\frac{9}{10} = \frac{x}{50}$ x = 45

B. $\frac{2}{3} = \frac{x}{18}$ x = 12 $\frac{3}{4} = \frac{x}{20}$ x = 15 $\frac{4}{7} = \frac{x}{28}$ x = 16

C. $\frac{3}{8} = \frac{x}{48}$ x = 18 $\frac{5}{2} = \frac{x}{10}$ x = 25 $\frac{1}{3} = \frac{x}{30}$ x = 10

D. $\frac{7}{3} = \frac{x}{18}$ x = 42 $\frac{7}{9} = \frac{x}{72}$ x = 56 $\frac{8}{9} = \frac{x}{36}$ x = 32

E. $\frac{2}{7} = \frac{x}{49}$ x = 14 $\frac{5}{8} = \frac{x}{64}$ x = 40 $\frac{9}{10} = \frac{x}{70}$ x = 63

19	20	[illegible]	63	31
16	13	40	29	12
15	42	23	45	10
14	37	25	11	5
43	18	56	32	17

What is it? ____________

 68 Maths, KS2

Page 67

Answer Key

Match Ups

Skill: Relating decimals and fractions

Name ____________________

Decimals can be used to show tenths. (0.6 = $\frac{6}{10}$) Write the decimals for the shaded parts.

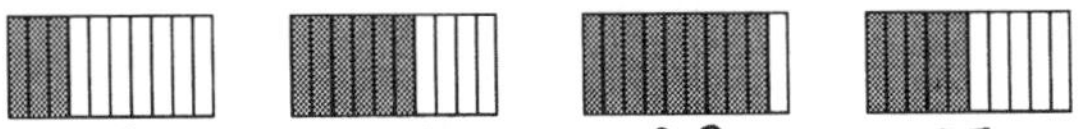

1. 0·3 2. 0·6 3. 0·9 4. 0·5

5. Match the decimals with the fractions and word names.

$\frac{8}{10}$	0.4	seven tenths
$\frac{1}{10}$	0.8	four tenths
$\frac{7}{10}$	0.1	eight tenths
$\frac{4}{10}$	0.7	one tenth

Whole numbers are shown before the decimal. Example: two and nine tenths = 2.9
Write the whole numbers and decimals for the shaded figures.

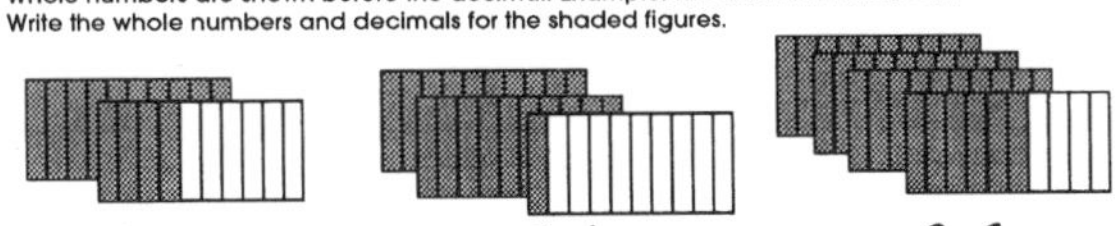

6. 1·4 7. 2·1 8. 3·6

Hundredths can be shown using decimals, too. twelve hundredths = 0.12

9. Match the decimals for the shaded parts.

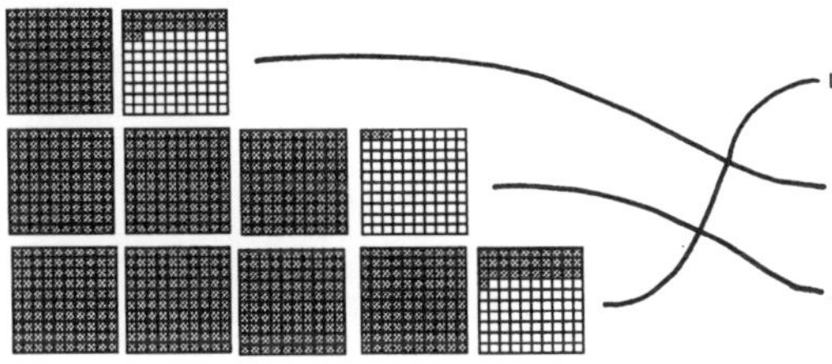

 69 Maths, KS2

Page 69

Decimal Dilemma

Skill: Writing and comparing decimals

Name ____________________

Write the decimals two other ways.

2.06	2 $\frac{6}{100}$	two and six hundredths
6.9	6 $\frac{9}{10}$	six and nine tenths
4.73	4 $\frac{73}{100}$	four and seventy-three hundredths
0.84	$\frac{84}{100}$	eighty-four hundredths
7.4	7 $\frac{4}{10}$	seven and four tenths

Circle the largest decimal in each section and draw a box around the smallest decimal. If the decimal circled is in the middle of the group, colour the section red. If it is on the right, colour it blue. If it is on the left, leave it white.

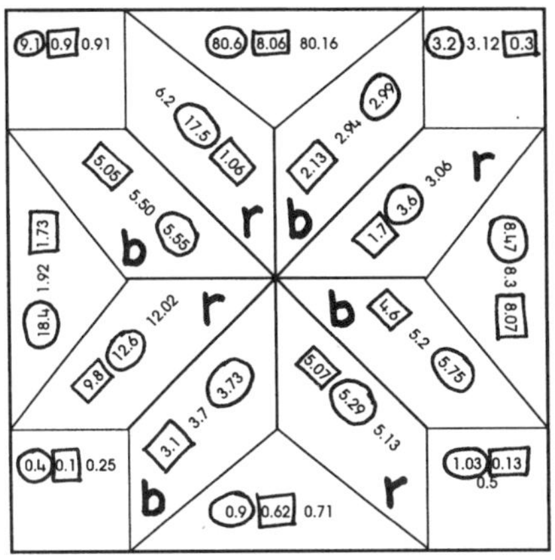

 70 Maths, KS2

Page 70

What's Missing?

Skill: Adding and subtracting decimals; comparing decimals

Name ____________________

Add or subtract.

A. 0.9 + 4.6 = 5.5; 5.7 − 2.9 = 2.8; 6.04 + 3.12 = 9.16; 5.55 − 4.60 = 0.95; 10.10 − 4.65 = 5.45; 11.7 + 10.1 = 21.8

B. 9.1 + 7.5 + 6.2 = 22.8; 51.6 + 27.9 + 18.8 = 98.3; 70.99 + 61.73 + 47.12 = 179.84; 18.4 + 20.7 + 32.5 = 71.6; 9.99 + 2.73 + 1.84 = 14.56; 6.71 + 12.58 + 9.01 = 28.30

C. 11.07 + 9.91 = 20.98 27.9 − 12.6 = 15.3 13.21 − 7.54 = 5.67

D. Write the missing digits.

4.36 + 5.74 = 10.10; 7.46 − 3.95 = 3.51; 8.44 + 5.66 = 14.10; 92.7 − 61.9 = 30.8; 79.9 − 38.3 = 41.6

E. 5.66 + 4.33 = 9.99 12.6 + 10.3 = 22.9

6.8 − 3.17 = 3.63

F. Shade in the boxes where the decimals are in numerical order.

4.9, 6.2	1.7, 1.6	12.06, 13.2
12.4, 9.6	8.0, 8.01	2.7, 2.67
5.01, 5.35	2.66, 2.65	72.9, 79.2
2.13, 2.03	1.6, 1.7	5.00, 4.9
2.04, 2.14	4.01, 4.00	18.6, 18.65
3.1, 3.01	9.9, 10.01	2.75, 2.70

 71 Maths, KS2

Page 71

Sweet Treats

Skill: Adding and subtracting decimals

Name ____________________

Add or subtract.

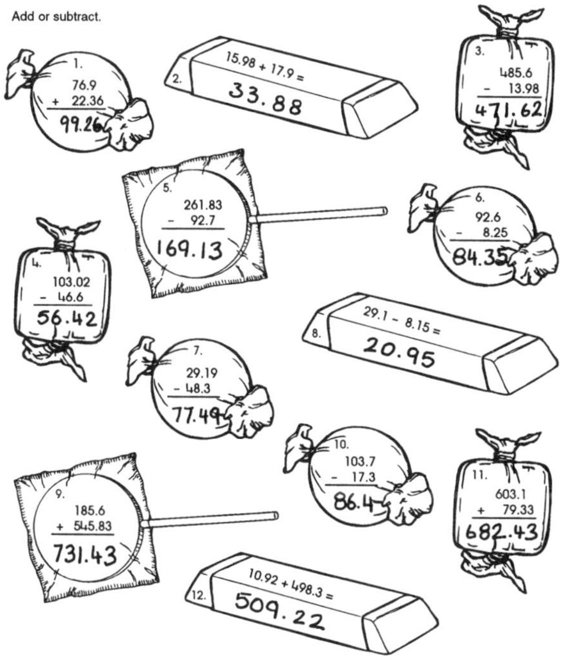

 72 Maths, KS2

Page 72

Answer Key

An Unusual Timepiece

Name ______________________

Skill: Fractions and percentages

Complete each equation with a ratio or a percentage. Use your answers to find a definition for "a unique timepiece."

A. $\frac{11}{100}$ = 11%	A. $\frac{8}{100}$ = 8%	A. $\frac{17}{100}$ = 17%	A. $\frac{25}{100}$ = 25%
A. $\frac{31}{100}$ = 31%	E. $\frac{43}{100}$ = 43%	E. $\frac{77}{100}$ = 77%	I. $\frac{49}{100}$ = 49%
I. $\frac{4}{100}$ = 4%	O. $\frac{19}{100}$ = 19%	O. $\frac{23}{100}$ = 23%	W. $\frac{46}{100}$ = 46%
G. $\frac{25}{100}$ = 25%	T. $\frac{33}{100}$ = 33%	D. $\frac{79}{100}$ = 79%	T. 14% = $\frac{14}{100}$
L. 67% = $\frac{67}{100}$	M. 58% = $\frac{58}{100}$	C. 53% = $\frac{53}{100}$	C. 28% = $\frac{28}{100}$
H. 12% = $\frac{12}{100}$	H. 71% = $\frac{71}{100}$	N. 17% = $\frac{17}{100}$	T. 39% = $\frac{39}{100}$
S. 84% = $\frac{84}{100}$	T. 47% = $\frac{47}{100}$		
D. 91% = $\frac{91}{100}$	G. 5% = $\frac{5}{100}$		
T. 75% = $\frac{75}{100}$			
L. 2% = $\frac{2}{100}$			

A WATCHDOG IS A DOG THAT CAN TELL TIME.

A	W	A	T	C	H	D	O	G
11%	46%	8%	$\frac{75}{100}$	$\frac{28}{100}$	$\frac{71}{100}$	79%	19%	$\frac{5}{100}$

I	S	A	D	O	G	T	H	A	T
49%	$\frac{84}{100}$	17%	$\frac{91}{100}$	23%	25%	$\frac{47}{100}$	$\frac{12}{100}$	25%	$\frac{39}{100}$

C	A	N	T	E	L	L	T	I	M	E
$\frac{53}{100}$	31%	$\frac{17}{100}$	33%	43%	$\frac{2}{100}$	$\frac{67}{100}$	$\frac{14}{100}$	4%	$\frac{58}{100}$	77%

Page 73

Perimeter Problems

Skill: Perimeter

Name ______________________

What is the highest waterfall in the world?

To find out, find the perimeter of each figure below at the bottom of the page. Write the letter that represents each problem above its answer.

Remember: Perimeter is equal to the sum of the sides of a figure.

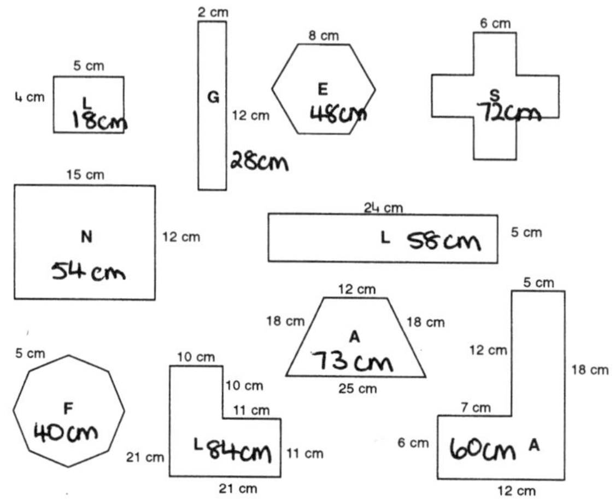

A	N	G	E	L	F	A	L	L	S
73 cm	54 cm	28 cm	48 cm	84 cm	40 cm	60 cm	18 cm	58 cm	72 cm

Page 74

Amazing Muscles

Skill: Area

Name ______________________

It takes 17 muscles to smile. How many muscles does it take to frown?

To find out, find the areas at the bottom of the page.
Write the letter that represents each problem above its answer.

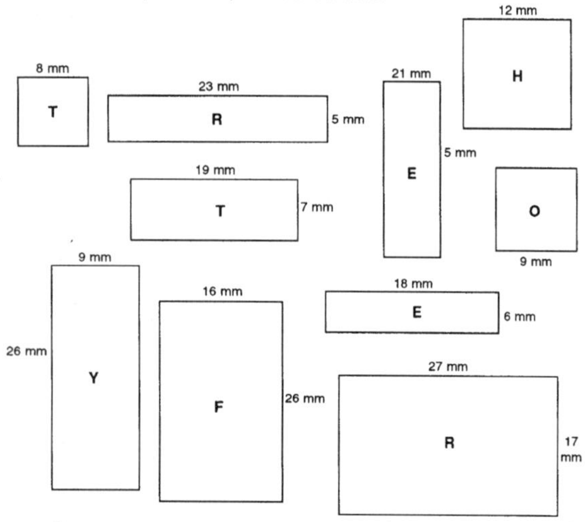

f	o	r	t	y	-	t	h	r	e	e
416 mm²	81 mm²	459 mm²	64 mm²	234 mm²		133 mm²	144 mm²	115 mm²	108 mm²	105 mm²

Page 75

Very Important Volume

Name ______________________

Skill: Volume

Volume is the number of cubic units that will fit inside a space figure. Build each figure below using linking cubes. Tell the number of cubes used.

1. 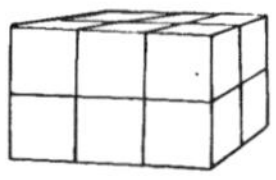

12 cubic units

2. 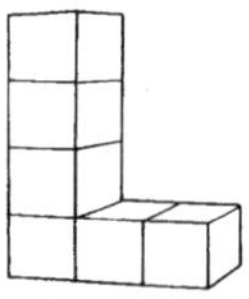

6 cubic units

3. 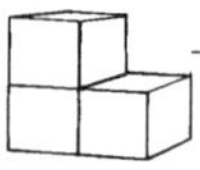

3 cubic units

Volume can be found by multiplying the length times the width times the height.

V = l x w x h

Find the volume of each figure below.

4. 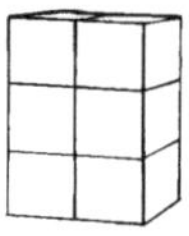

2 x 1 x 3 = 6 cu. units

5. 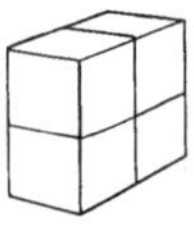

1 x 2 x 2 = 4 cu. units

6. 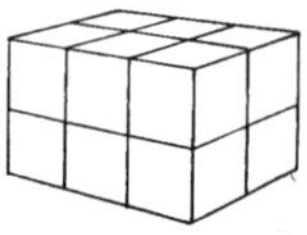

3 x 2 x 2 = 12 cu. units

7. 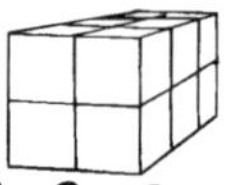

2 x 3 x 2 = 12 cu. units

8. 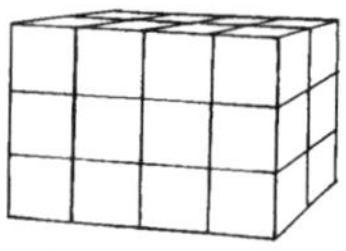

4 x 2 x 3 = 24 cu. units

9. 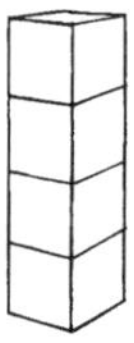

1 x 1 x 4 = 4 cu. units

Page 76

Answer Key

How Hot Is It?

Skill: Temperature - Celsius, Fahrenheit

Name ______________________

Temperature is measured in degrees Celsius or Fahrenheit.

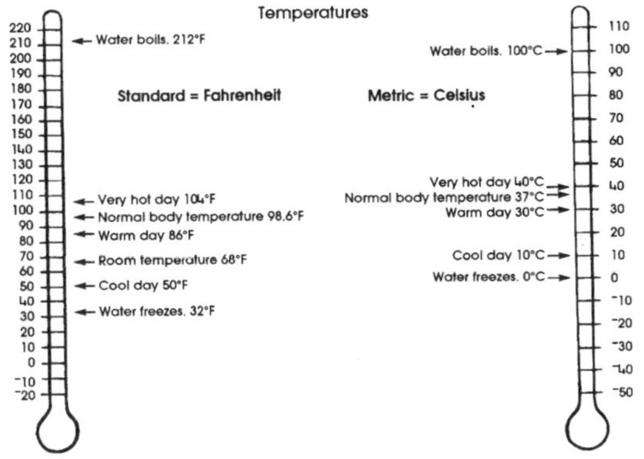

Use the thermometers to show the temperatures below in Celsius and Fahrenheit.

	degrees Fahrenheit	degrees Celsius
Water boils.	212	100
Normal body temperature	98.6	37
A very hot day	104	40
A warm day	86	30
A cool day	50	10
Water freezes.	32	0

Page 77

Quadrilateral Riddles

Skill: Quadrilaterals

Name ______________________

Solve each riddle. Then draw it on the geoboard dot paper grids. Use the Word Bank to help you.

Word Bank

kite parallelogram rectangle rhombus square trapezium

1. I have 2 pairs of parallel sides and 2 pairs of congruent angles. I have no right angles. What am I? parallelogram
2. I have only one pair of parallel sides. What am I? trapezium
3. I have 2 pairs of parallel sides. All 4 of my sides are the same length, but I have no right angles. What am I? rhombus
4. I have 2 pairs of parallel sides. Each pair of sides is a different length. All 4 of my angles are right angles. What am I? rectangle
5. I have 2 pairs of touching sides the same length. None of my angles are right angles. What am I? kite
6. I have 2 pairs of parallel sides, and all of my sides are the same length. All 4 of my angles have the same measure. What am I? square

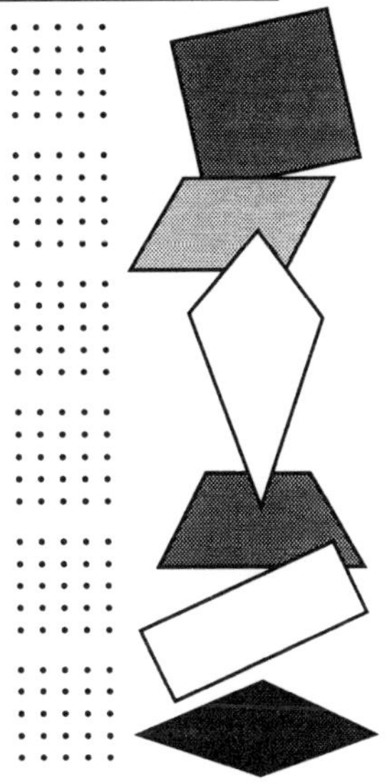

Page 78

In Shape

Skill: Geometric shapes

Name ______________________

Match the names with the shapes.

Plane Figures

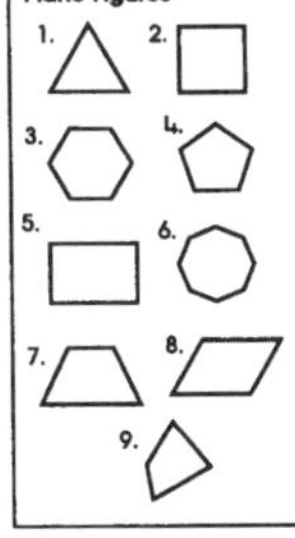

3 hexagon
2 square
5 rectangle
6 octagon
8 parallelogram
1 triangle
4 pentagon
7 trapezium
9 quadrilateral

Space Figures

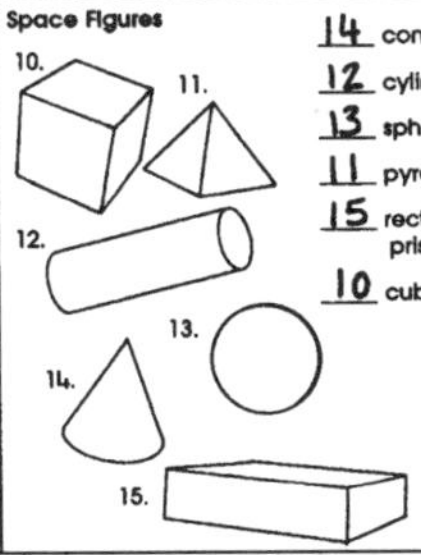

14 cone
12 cylinder
13 sphere
11 pyramid
15 rectangular prism
10 cube

16. On a separate sheet of paper, draw a picture that contains at least one of every figure. Label the figures.

Each flat surface is a *face*. Two faces meet at an *edge*. Three (or more) edges meet at a *vertex*. Label the parts shown.

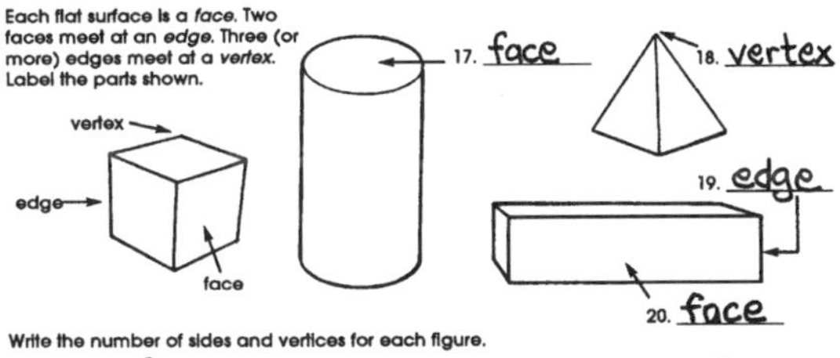

Write the number of sides and vertices for each figure.

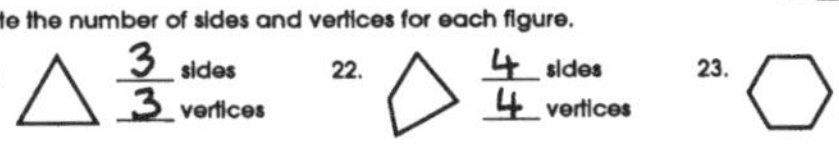

21. 3 sides, 3 vertices
22. 4 sides, 4 vertices
23. 6 sides, 6 vertices

Page 79

It's the Same

Skill: Congruency; symmetry; circles

Name ______________________

A. Congruent figures have the same size and shape. Colour the congruent figures.

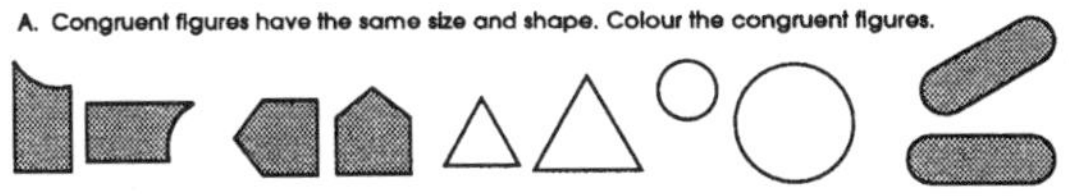

B. A line of symmetry divides a shape into congruent shapes. Colour only the figures with lines of symmetry.

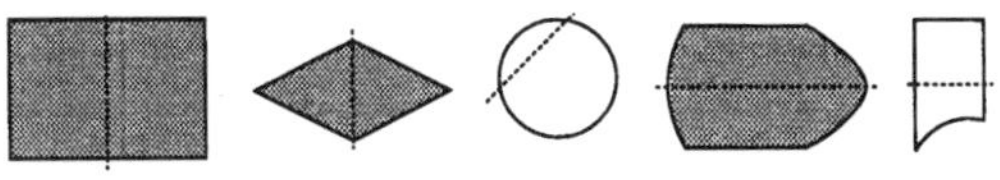

C. Use a ruler to draw two sets of congruent figures. Then draw two figures, each with a line of symmetry.

Congruent Figures	Symmetry
Answers	vary

D.

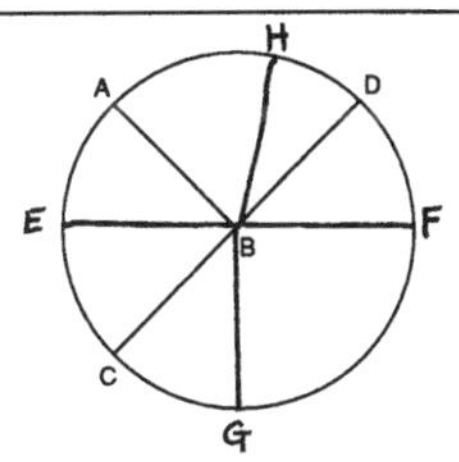

1. A circle is named by its centre. This circle is B.
2. Name 2 radii. BA BC or BD
3. Name a diameter. CD
4. Draw another diameter using a red pencil or crayon. Label it EF.
5. Draw two radii using a blue crayon. Label them BG and BH.

Page 80

Answer Key

Congruent or Similar?

Name ______________________

Skill: Congruence and similarity

Decide if the figures below are congruent or similar.
If they are congruent, colour the figures yellow.
If they are similar, colour the figures blue.
If they are not congruent or similar, colour the figures red.

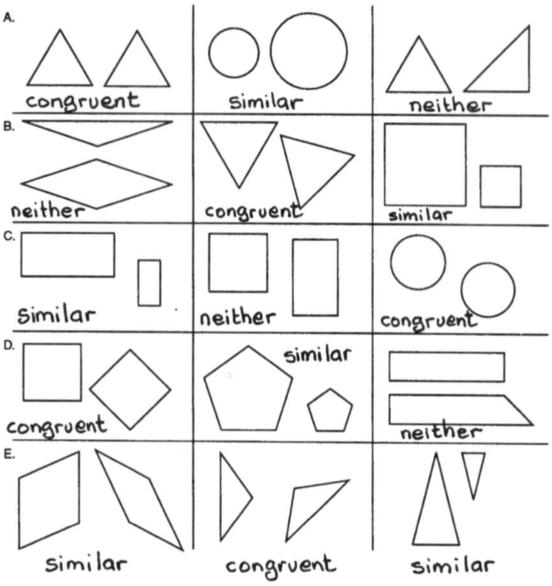

Page 81

Angles and Lines

Name ______________________

Skill: Lines and angles

Acute angles measure less than 90°.
Right angles measure 90°.
Obtuse angles measure more than 90° but less than 180°.
Parallel lines never intersect.
Perpendicular lines intersect at 90° angles.

Use the figure below to answer the questions.

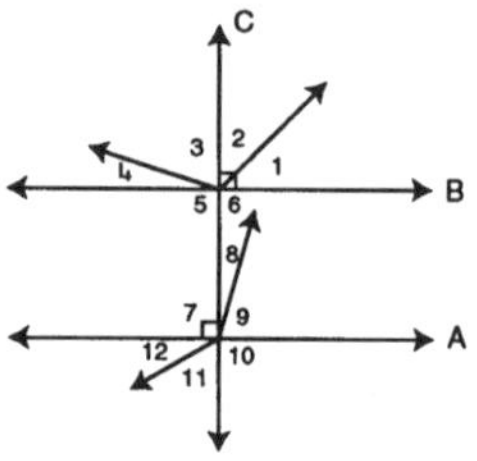

1. Name a pair of parallel lines. B and A
2. Name four acute angles. 1, 2, 3, 4 also 8, 9, 11, 12
3. Name two right angles. 5, 6 also 7, 10
4. Name a pair of perpendicular lines. C and B also C and A
5. Angle 11 is a(n) acute angle.
6. Angle 7 plus angle 8 make a(n) obtuse angle.
7. Line A is perpendicular to line C.
8. Angle 1 plus angle 2 make a(n) right angle.
9. Draw an obtuse angle.
10. Draw a right angle.
11. Draw an acute angle.

Page 82

Angling for an Answer

Name ______________________

Skill: Measuring angles

Measure each angle. Use your answers and the code to solve the following riddle:

What is black and white and read all over?

A = 75°
A = 110°
E = 95°
E = 20°
N = 150°
P = 45°
P = 130°
R = 90°
S = 55°
W = 40°

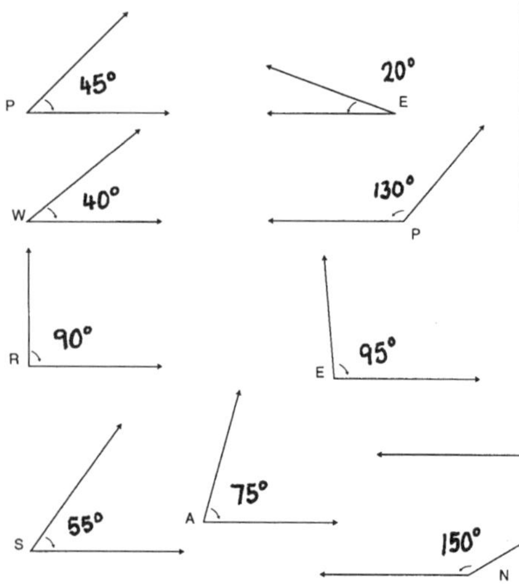

A (110°) N (150°) E (20°) W (40°) S (55°) P (45°) A (75°) P (130°) E (95°) R (90°)

Page 83

Bits and Pieces

Name ______________________

Skill: Triangles

The angles below can be combined to form four triangles. Use the letters to name each triangle.

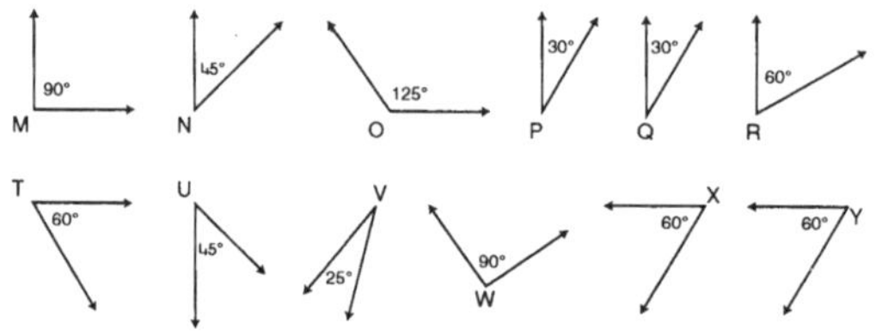

Triangle 1: MTP
Triangle 2: OVQ
Triangle 3: RXY
Triangle 4: NUW

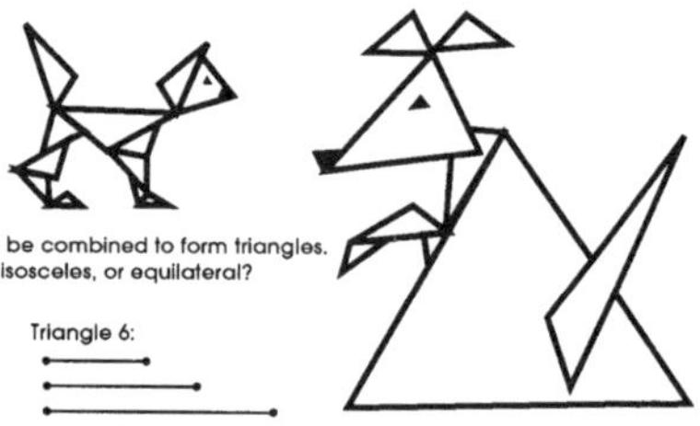

The line segments below can be combined to form triangles. Will the triangles be scalene, isosceles, or equilateral?

Triangle 5: isosceles
Triangle 6: scalene
Triangle 7: equilateral
Triangle 8: scalene
Triangle 9: isosceles

Page 84

Answer Key

What's On?

Skill: Charts

Name ____________________

You can find out many things from charts and schedules.
Read the television schedule below and answer the questions.

Saturday Morning TV Guide

Channel	6:00 a.m.	6:30 a.m.	7:00 a.m.	7:30 a.m.	8:00 a.m.	8:30 a.m.
1	Field Trip	Growing Up	Animal Fun	Puppy Pride	Cars and Trucks	Turtle Time
2	Dragon Ball	Mice From Mars	Today in Town	Fantastic Fred	Giant Spiders	Harry the Hippo
3	Nosey News	Call It	Strong Man	Wonderman	Candy	Time for Fun
4	Creature Fun	Girl Time	Adventures of Wild Warriors	Sing Me a Song		Feed the Children
5	Jellybean Jam	News Time	Masked Ranger	Tommy's Castle	Ranger Rovers	Attack of Killer Tomatoes
6				Reading for Fun	Friendly Fun	Where is Jimmy?

1. What time does the first show start? *6:00 am*
2. What time will you need to be awake to watch "Growing Up?" *6:30am*
   What channel is it on? *1*
3. What time will you be able to see "Adventures of Wild Warriors?" *7:00 am*
4. What show follows "Adventures of Wild Warriors" on the same channel? *Sing me a song*
   How long will it last? *1 hour*
5. What channel must you watch to learn more about reading? *6*
6. Why wouldn't you already be watching that channel? *not on air until 7:30am*
7. At what time do you change channels to see "Turtle Time?" *8:30am*
   What channel is it on? *1*

Copyright © 1999 Brighter Vision Education Ltd — 85 — Maths, KS2

Page 85

Graphs, Graphs, Graphs

Skill: Line and bar graphs

Name ____________________

There are many different ways to show information on graphs. Read each graph below and answer the questions. The temperature scale is in Fahrenheit.

This Week's Temperatures

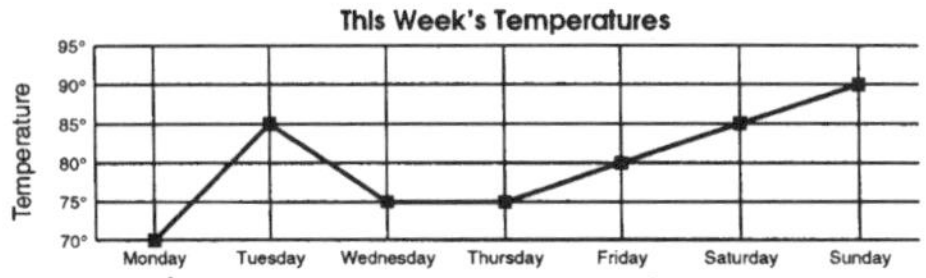

This is a *line* graph.

1. *sunday* was the warmest day. It was *90* degrees.
2. What two days had the same cool temperature? *wednesday thursday*
3. Is the temperature rising or going down? *rising*
4. What day was the coolest day? *monday*
   What was the temperature? *70°*
5. What was the difference in temperature between Monday and Sunday? *20°*
6. What two days had the same warm temperature? *tuesday saturday*

How Do People Like Their Ice Cream?

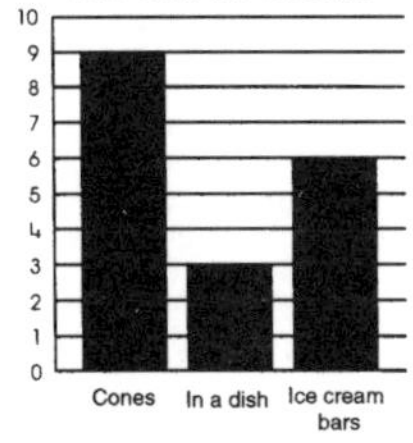

This is a *bar* graph.

7. How many more people prefer cones to bars? *3*
8. How many less people prefer a dish of ice cream than a cone? *6*
9. What do people prefer the most? *cones*
10. How many people were asked? *18*
11. How many people like cones and bars? *15*
12. How many people like a dish of ice cream and bars? *9*

Copyright © 1999 Brighter Vision Education Ltd — 86 — Maths, KS2

Page 86

Favourite Fun

Skill: Circle graphs; making graphs

Name ____________________

Favourite Classes

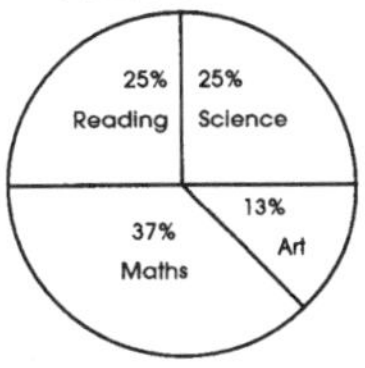

This is a *pie* graph.

Use the graph to answer the questions below. The graph represents 32 students' favourite classes.

1. What class is liked the most? *maths*
   What is the percentage? *37%*
2. What two classes are liked the same? *reading science*
   What is the percentage? *25%*
3. What is the total percentage of all the classes? *100*
4. What class is liked the least? *art*
5. How many students liked reading the best? *8*

Make a line graph and a bar graph using the information below. Don't forget to label each side of the graphs and then give the graphs titles.

Students were asked what their favourite type of book to read was. The response was as follows:

12 liked sports.
8 liked science fiction.
10 liked history.
5 liked mystery.
5 liked riddles.

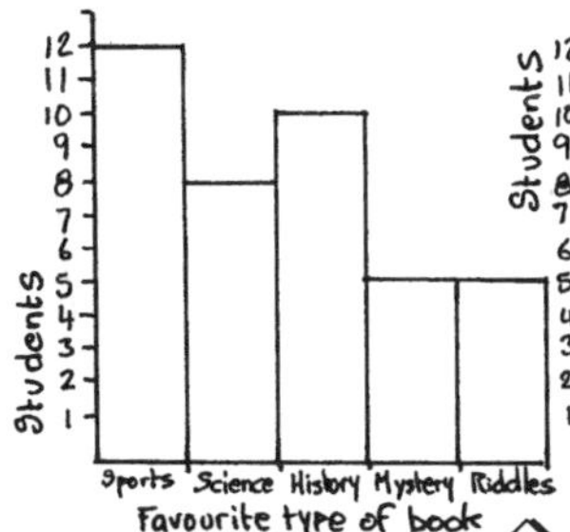

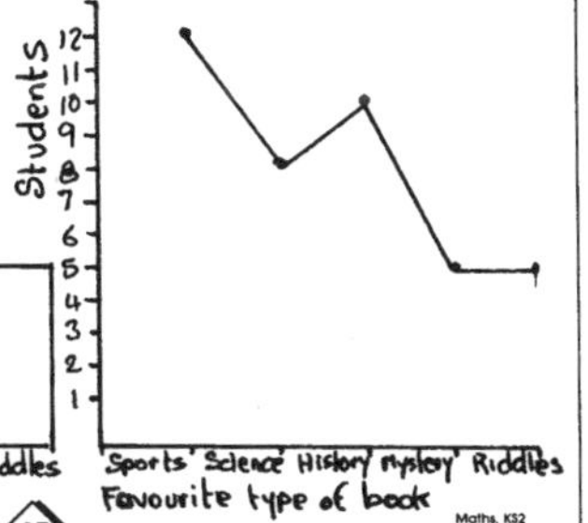

Copyright © 1999 Brighter Vision Education Ltd — 87 — Maths, KS2

Page 87

No Bones About It!

Skill: Co-ordinates graph

Name ____________________

What is the largest bone in your body?

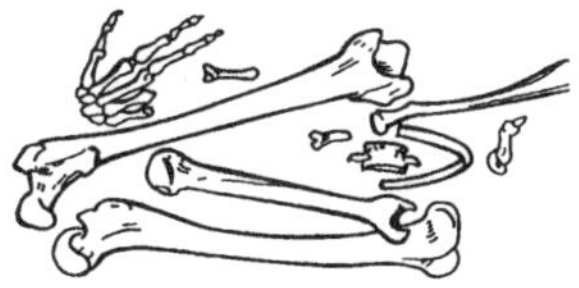

Find the points at the bottom of the page on the graph. Write the letter that represents each point above its ordered pair to find the answer to the riddle.

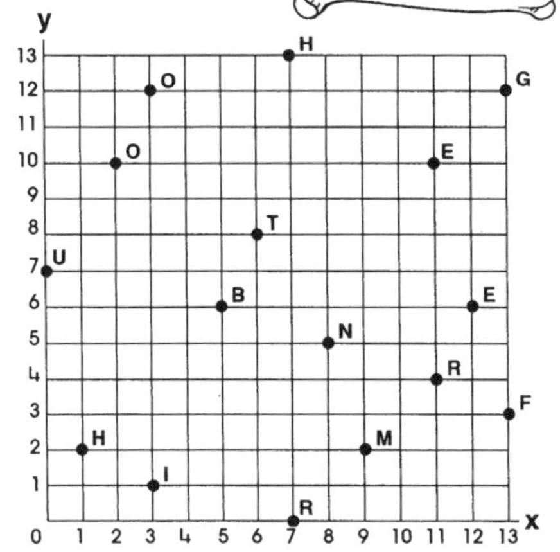

t (6, 8) *h* (1, 2) *i* (3, 1) *g* (13, 12) *h* (7, 13) *b* (5, 6) *o* (3, 12) *n* (8, 5) *e* (12, 6)

(*o* (2, 10) *r* (11, 4) *f* (13, 3) *e* (11, 10) *m* (9, 2) *u* (0, 7) *r* (7, 0))

Copyright © 1999 Brighter Vision Education Ltd — 88 — Maths, KS2

Page 88

Answer Key

Game Time

Name ______________________

Skill: Addition key words, Addition facts 11-18

These key words are often clues that tell you to add. Use them to help you solve addition problems.

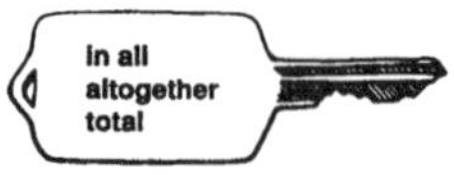

Read each problem below. Underline the key words. Then write the number sentence and the answer.

1. Four friends were playing a game. Mai counted 5 question cards. Zach counted 7. How many question cards did they count in all? 5+7=12 — 12 question cards	2. There are 6 bonus cards to place near "Start" and 8 bonus cards to place near the dragon. How many bonus cards are there in all? 6+8=14 — 14 bonus cards
3. Mai's first card let her move ahead 3 spaces. Her second card let her move ahead 9. What was the total number of spaces Mai moved? 3+9=12 — 12 spaces	4. Ricky's first card let him skip ahead 4 spaces. His second card let him move ahead 8. How many spaces did Ricky move altogether? 4+8=12 — 12 spaces
5. Zach could win if he could get an 8 and a 7 on his next two cards. What is the total number of points Zach needs to win? 8+7=15 — 15 points	6. Lydia won the game. She moved ahead 9 and then 7 spaces. How many spaces did she move altogether in her last two turns? 9+7=16 — 16 spaces

Brainwork! Write three addition word problems about a game. Use different key words in each. Ask a friend to solve them.

 89 Maths, KS2

Page 89

Too Many Pets

Name ______________________

Skill: 2-digit subtraction

Write the number sentence and answer.

	1. Mary had 26 goldfish. The cat ate 12. How many does Mary have now? 26 - 12 = 14 — Mary has 14 goldfish.
2. John caught 38 lizards. 15 of them got away. How many lizards are left? 38 - 15 = 23 — John has 23 lizards left.	3. Sue had 14 cats. She gave 12 of them to a friend. How many cats does Sue have now? 14 - 12 = 2 — Sue has 2 cats now.
4. Jim had 29 baby hamsters. He gave 14 to a pet shop. How many does he have left? 29 - 14 = 15 — Jim has 15 hamsters left.	5. Bill had 45 rabbits. He sold 25 of them. How many does he have now? 45 - 25 = 20 — Bill has 20 rabbits now.

 90 Maths, KS2

Page 90

It's Your Birthday!

Name ______________________

Skill: Comparisons 11-18

Write the number sentence and answer.

1. Ann is 11 years old. Her sister is 3. How much older is Ann than her sister? 11-3=8 — 8 years older.	2. John is 16 years old. Bill is 7. How much older is John than Bill? 16-7=9 — 9 years older.
3. Jim is 11 years old. Frank is 9. How much younger is Frank than Jim? 11-9=2 — 2 years younger.	4. If Mike is 14 and Nancy is 9, how much older is Mike than Nancy? 14-9=5 — 5 years older.
5. Jeff, who is 13 years old, has a brother who is 6. How much younger is Jeff's brother? 13-6=7 — 7 years younger.	

 91 Maths, KS2

Page 91

Cross-Numeral Puzzle

Name ______________________

Skill: Review

ACROSS		DOWN	
A.	465 + 327	A.	939 - 224
F.	824 - 619	B.	158 + 96
G.	700 - 215	C.	7,496 + 5,367
I.	6,521 - 2,843	D.	8,064 + 7,296
J.	2,774 + 984	E.	57 + 83 + 220
K.	872 - 218	H.	29 + 68 + 353
M.	198 + 258	L.	3,000 - 2,518
N.	37 + 164	M.	219 + 212

 92 Maths, KS2

Page 92

Answer Key

Puzzling Problems

Name ______________________ Skill: Dividing by 2- and 3-digit numbers

Use the clues to solve the puzzle.

ACROSS

A. 6,048 ÷ 12 = 504
C. 14,848 ÷ 16 = 928
E. 31,680 ÷ 6 = 5280
G. 7,056 ÷ 84 = 84
I. 0 ÷ 36 = 0
J. 98,593 ÷ 11 = 8963
M. 5,240 ÷ 10 = 524
N. 948 ÷ 12 = 79
Q. 6,630 ÷ 17 = 390
R. 6,240 ÷ 20 = 312
S. 13,000 ÷ 25 = 520

DOWN

A. 11,776 ÷ 2 = 5888
B. 2,070 ÷ 46 = 45
C. 8,901 ÷ 9 = 989
D. 1,780 ÷ 89 = 20
F. 31,276 ÷ 14 = 2234
H. 6,435 ÷ 13 = 495
K. 68,992 ÷ 11 = 6272
L. 11,376 ÷ 3 = 3792
O. 9,000 ÷ 10 = 900
P. 2,211 ÷ 67 = 33
Q. 875 ÷ 25 = 35

A 5	0	B 4	■	C 9	D 2	8
8	■	E 5	F 2	8	0	■
G 8	H 4	■	2	9	■	I 0
J 8	9	K 6	3	■	L 3	
■	M 5	2	4	■	N 7	O 9
P 3		7	■	Q 3	9	0
R 3	1	2	■	S 5	2	0

Page 93

Make a Million

Name ______________________ Skill: Critical thinking

Complete each problem so that the sum is one million.

A.
237,512 + 762,488 = 1,000,000
456,897 + 543,103 = 1,000,000
79,936 + 920,064 = 1,000,000
615,793 + 384,207 = 1,000,000

B.
564,216 + 435,784 = 1,000,000
935,142 + 64,858 = 1,000,000
900,616 + 99,384 = 1,000,000
499,999 + 500,001 = 1,000,000

C.
424,116 + 514,352 + 61,532 = 1,000,000
492,075 + 384,109 + 123,816 = 1,000,000
82,936 + 426,817 + 490,247 = 1,000,000
496,385 + 287,196 + 216,419 = 1,000,000

D.
369,804 + 64,039 + 566,157 = 1,000,000
25,519 + 664,819 + 309,662 = 1,000,000
831,678 + 138,508 + 29,814 = 1,000,000
23,182 + 976,596 + 222 = 1,000,000

999,998 999,999...

Write two problems of your own that have sums of one million.

E. ______ + ______ = 1,000,000

F. ______ + ______ = 1,000,000

Page 94

Run for Fun and Fitness

Name ______________________ Skill: Problem solving with fractions

Anna and Robyn run every day. They record their distances in a table.

Running Log (in miles)

Day	Monday	Tuesday	Wednesday	Thursday	Friday
Anna	3 1/2	4 3/4	3 1/2	5	5 3/4
Robyn	3 7/8	4	4 1/4	4 7/8	5 5/8

Solve. Write addition or subtraction equations to help you.

1. How far did Anna run on Monday and Tuesday? $8\frac{1}{4}$
2. How far did Robyn run on Wednesday and Thursday? $9\frac{1}{8}$
3. On which day was Robyn and Anna's combined distance least? greatest? least = Monday greatest = Friday
4. Who ran further on Monday? By how many miles? Robyn $\frac{3}{8}$ of a mile
5. Who ran further on Thursday? By how many miles? Anna $\frac{1}{8}$ of a mile
6. Estimate the total number of miles run by each runner for the five-day period. 23 miles
7. On which day did Anna and Robyn run a total of about 10 miles? Thursday
8. On which day did Robyn run more than 1/2 mile farther than Anna? Wednesday

Page 95

Super Sentences

Name ______________________ Skill: Adding fractions with unlike denominators

Complete the number sentences below. Simplify all answers.

$\frac{2}{3}$	+	$\frac{14}{15}$	=	$1\frac{3}{5}$
+	■	+		
$\frac{1}{30}$	+	$\frac{1}{6}$	=	$\frac{1}{5}$
=		=		+
$\frac{7}{10}$		$1\frac{1}{10}$		$\frac{1}{40}$
				=
$\frac{1}{8}$	+	$\frac{1}{10}$	=	$\frac{9}{40}$
+	■	+		
$\frac{1}{4}$	+	$\frac{1}{5}$	=	$\frac{9}{20}$
=	■	=	■	+
$\frac{3}{8}$	+	$\frac{3}{10}$	=	$\frac{27}{40}$
				=
				$1\frac{1}{8}$

Page 96

Answer Key

Puzzling Problems

Skill: Percentage of a number

Name ______________________

Find the percent problems. Use your answers to solve the puzzle.

ACROSS

A. 10% of 100 = 10
B. 20% of 125 = 25
D. 33 1/3% of 135 = 45
E. 66 2/3% of 75 = 50
F. 50% of 130 = 65
G. 15% of 500 = 75
H. 5% of 16,000 = 800
I. 25% of 360 = 90
J. 10% of 150 = 15
L. 20% of 150 = 30
M. 50% of 90 = 45
N. 50% of 1,120 = 560
P. 25% of 280 = 70
Q. 50% of 160 = 80
R. 20% of 450 = 90

DOWN

A. 20% of 75 = 15
B. 40% of 50 = 20
C. 50% of 750 = 375
D. 5% of 8,000 = 400
E. 10% of 550 = 55
F. 25% of 2,500 = 625
G. 66 2/3% of 105 = 70
H. 50% of 170 = 85
I. 25% of 380 = 95
J. 1% of 10,000 = 100
K. 50% of 450 = 225
L. 25% of 140 = 35
M. 80% of 50 = 40
O. 80% of 750 = 600
P. 50% of 140 = 70
Q. 25% of 340 = 85

Page 97

Euler's Law

Skill: Faces, edges and vertices

Name ______________________

Complete the table to learn about Euler's Law.

Space Figure	Vertices	Faces	Sum of vertices and faces	Edges
1. 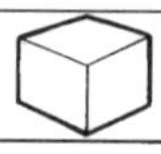	8	6	14	12
2. 	6	5	11	9
3. 	5	5	10	8
4. 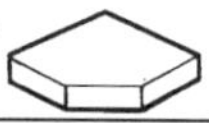	10	7	17	15
5. 	8	6	14	12
6. 	6	6	12	10
7. 	4	4	8	6

What do you notice about the sum of the faces and vertices and the number of edges in each figure?

THE NUMBER OF EDGES IS TWO LESS THAN THE SUM OF VERTICES AND FACES

Page 98